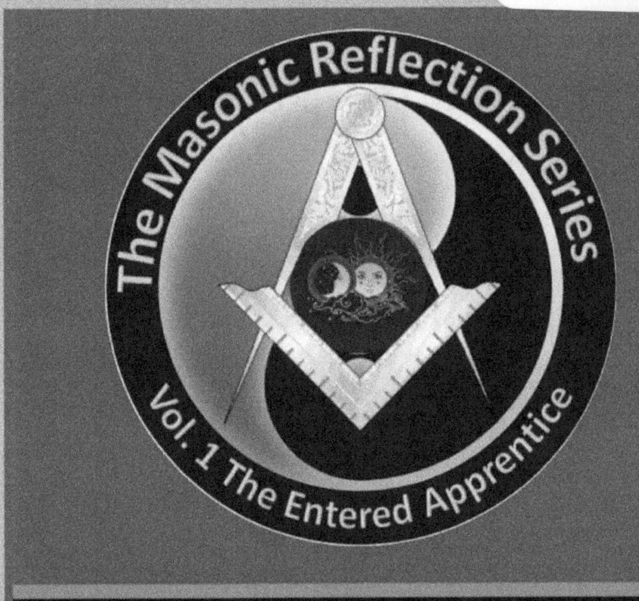

Reflections Of An Entered Apprentice

Bro. Tony Pedroza 33°
"The Quarryman"

Dedicated to the Memory of

C.J. Peck
&
Roosevelt Tennessee

Your lights shine brighter than ever!

R.I.P.

Special Thanks to my mentors

The Vapor
"Who is everywhere and nowhere."

The Banker

The Snowman

The Truck Driver
Who drives from "The Root To The Fruit."

Mr. Circumpunct
"The True Ambassador to Duality"

The Liberian Reflection

1- The Symbolism of The Entered Apprentice Degree

The Entered Apprentice is aimed in its symbolic meaning to provide a representation of a child just arriving at the struggles, worries, and responsibilities of an earthly and accountable reality.

On his entrance into the Lodge, the candidate is reminded of the weak and helpless state of man on his entry into the world unprepared for the demands of the present, unaware of the differences of the future, and reliant on his wellbeing and the very existence of the Grand Architect of the Universe in whom alone, in all trials and difficulties, there is confident and long-lasting trust.

And as the youth is prepared by a proper and moral education for his journey through life, the Apprentice finds in this degree those first instructions whereon to construct his future morals and Masonic construction.

He now receives the basic details of that universal language. Hereafter, he is to communicate with his brethren of all nations, to understand and be understood by Masons of every language and dialect under the sun.

He is instructed to take, as a baton and scrip for his passage, an understanding of all the virtues that spread out the heart and dignify the soul.

<u>Concealment</u>, <u>duty</u>, <u>humility</u>, trust in <u>The Grand Architect of
the Universe</u>, the innocence of assumptions, and the economy
of time, are all taught by symbolic ceremonies too inspiring
in their character ever to be forgotten. And, lastly, as charity
forms the chief cornerstone of all the Masonic virtues, the
beauty, and holiness of this attribute are described
in emblematic forms which no spoken language could equal.
This degree of Entered Apprentice is, in short, one of
probation and preparation for a higher position and more
glorious privileges and duties. *ALBERT MACKEY*

ENTERED
APPRENTICE

CAUTION

Disclaimer:

The term "ignorance" (*lacking the search for knowledge*) is used in this book as opposed to "intellect."(*seeking-knowledge*)

The term "unworthy" (*unstudied or unread*) is used in this book as opposed to "worthy."(*studied or well-read*)

Definitions: Merriam-Webster Dictionary

Ignorance: *the state or fact of being ignorant: lack of knowledge, education, or awareness*

Unworthy: *lacking in excellence or value, not meritorious, not deserved, inappropriate to one's condition or station*

Masonic Definitions:

Mackey's Encyclopedia and Macoy's Cyclopedia

Ignorance is Darkness in Masonry: *Darkness has, in all the systems of initiation, been deemed a symbol of ignorance and so opposed to light, which is the symbol of knowledge. Hence the rule that the eye should not see until the heart has conceived the true nature of those beauties which constitute the mysteries of the Order. In the Ancient Mysteries, the candidate was always shrouded in darkness as a preparatory step to the reception of the full light of knowledge.*

Unworthy: *Those whose lives and characters reflect no credit on the Institution, whose ears turn coldly from its beautiful lessons of morality, whose hearts are untouched by its soothing influences of brotherly kindness, whose hands are not opened to aid in its deeds of charity is a fact which we cannot deny, although we may be permitted to express our grief while we acknowledge its truth.*

Though in the Temple, they are not of the Temple; they are among us; but are not with us; they belong to our household, but they are not of our conviction. Attempts to teach them, but they refuse to be instructed; seeing, they have not perceived; and hearing, they have not understood the symbolic language in which our lessons of wisdom are communicated. The fault is not with us that we have not given, but with them, that they have not received.

Reflecting on the Hidden Mysteries of
Ancient Freemasonry
(The Art, The Part, The Point)

THE ART L
Merriam-Webster Dictionary defines "Art": *1- skill acquired by experience, study, or observation; 2- a branch of learning: one of the humanities arts plural (LIBERAL ARTS):3- an occupation requiring knowledge or skill.*

Masonry defines *"The Art" of the Mysteries of Masonry as " arts meaning the knowledge or things made known, revealed or unveiled" (Mackey's Encyclopedia, History of Freemasonry, and Macoy's Cyclopedia)*

As I reflect on the Mysteries of Masonry, I cannot help but think back to how I was taught to read as a child, from left to right and top to bottom—two different directions that lead to something unique and meaningful: learning.

I remember getting excited and fascinated with learning as a child. Reading left to right as if to form an imaginary horizontal Line ─. From top to bottom, as if to create an imaginary perpendicular line | as both come together to form a right angle of 90°. | + ─ = Г or *(NE corner)*

It came to me that learning the "Art" portion of the Mysteries of Masonry is parallel to a horizontal and a perpendicular line or as learning to read from left to right and top to bottom *(southern point of view or a clock 9-3 or west to east).*

I viewed it from a cardinal direction perspective, as I learned from the west to the east or even sunset to sunrise or darkness to light. And for what purpose?

Having received in elementary school basic knowledge about the north, south, east, and west or cardinal directions and how the sunrises in the east and sets in the west, along with noon or meridian being the brightest time of day.

These were all things I remember reading and learning in elementary school. I have come to understand that reading using horizontal movements and perpendicular directions is all about knowledge and wisdom.

The more I read, the more I learned, the more I learned, the more wisdom I gained; it seems very simple. Finally, it dawned on me that the more I read and understood the information provided in the Entered Apprentice Degree, the verbal and the non-verbal, the more apparent things became.

The more I practice (*gaining knowledge and wisdom*), that I create a **parallel** with a mystical journey traveling from the west to the east or from sunset *(darkness)* to sunrise *(light)* or just a horizontal line, but why?

Simply put, the "Art' portion of the Mysteries of Masonry was about reading, reciting, practicing, and learning the hidden meanings, the veiled and the allegories.

Nothing more than a ***triple*** journey of the physical action of reading (*obtaining knowledge*), the mental activity of Intellectual growth (gaining wisdom) and behavioral actions (movements) of spiritual growth.

Almost like searching for the perfect triune or trinity. So now "whence came you" and "wither you traveling" are clear and transparent to me; it's about reading to learn, learning to know, and knowing to change behavior and grow.

Or the beauty of learning, the strength of knowing, and the wisdom to evolve or elevate. My conductor instilled in us the importance that as we spoke with some of the well-informed brethren of the lodge, we learned that there are many masons out there.

Since we did not know them all, they did not know us. How are they to know us as masons, and conversely, how are we to know them to be masons? Hence, as Entered Apprentices, we needed to know and learn all the craftsmanship and knowledge in this degree.

At that moment, I understood the importance and vital interest to all brethren that the Entered Apprentices know their craft. They may find it necessary to prove themselves to us as we may need to prove ourselves to them.

Imagine how incomplete a man can feel or be seen if he does not know his craft or cannot hold a thorough masonic conversation with other masons. It is of interest to everyone in the lodge that the Entered Apprentices know their craft and be well versed and show proficiency.

The Entered Apprentice should be not only willing but enthusiastically eager to learn what is required because of its effect upon his future Masonic career.

As a Master Mason, when I am the Conductor, and if my EAs are not motivated, enthusiastic, and eager to learn, the problem is not them. The problem falls on me, the conductor; am I worthy and well qualified, duly, and truly prepared to be a Conductor?

How can we expect EAs to be motivated and enthusiastic if we are less motivated, enthusiastic, eager to teach, and proficient in our craft?

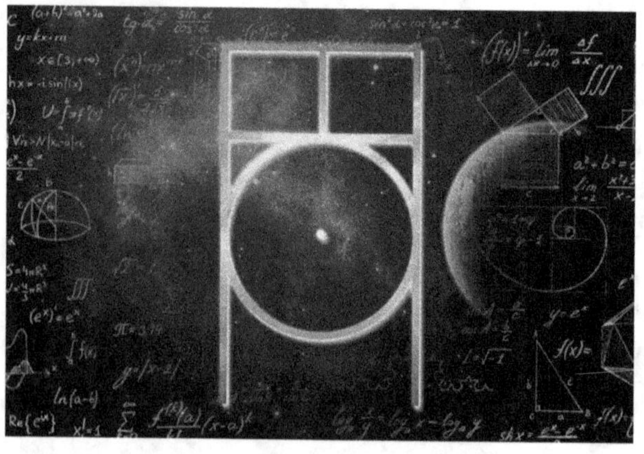

As Speculative Freemasonry builds only character, a feeling of unworthiness is as much a handicap in lodge life as a piece of faulty stone is in building a wall. But the most important reason for learning the work thoroughly goes further. It applies more and more as the Fellowcraft's Degree is reached and passed and is most vital after the initiate has the proud right to say, "I am a Master Mason." **(Claudy)**

Reflecting on the Hidden Mysteries of Ancient Freemasonry (The Art, The Part, The Point)

The Part —

Merriam-Webster Dictionary defines "Part"*: 1- one of the often indefinite or unequal subdivisions into which something is or is regarded as divided and which together constitute the whole.*

Masonry defines *"**The Part**" of the Mysteries of Masonry as "the degrees into which Masonry is divided" (Mackey's Encyclopedia, History of Freemasonry, and Macoy's Cyclopedia)*

The Entered Apprentice Degree has two divisions, **The Initiation** *(includes Open & Close)* and The **Lectures** *(includes symbolism and charge).*

The Initiation:

Merriam-Webster Dictionary defines "Initiation"*: **1a** the act or an instance of initiating. **B:** the process of being initiated; **C:** the rites, ceremonies, trials, or instructions with which one is made a member of a group or society or is invested with a particular function or status **2:** the condition of being initiated into some experience or sphere of Activity: KNOWLEDGEABLENESS*

Masonry defines *"**The Initiation**"* as "It is derived from the word 'initia," *which signifies the first principles of science. Freemasons have adopted the word to signify a reception into their Order. It is sometimes specially applied to the reception into the First Degree, but he who has been made an Entered Apprentice is more correctly said to be Entered"* (Mackey's Encyclopedia, History of Freemasonry, and Macoy's Cyclopedia)

The initiation is made up of fourteen distinct "acts" in two series of seven each: the first seven are in a State of Darkness (*intellectual ignorance*); the second seven are in a State of Light (*intellectual introduction*), which corresponds to the Ancient Mysteries.

The first seven are Preparation, Alarm, Received, Invoking, Traveling, Stations, and Covenant. The second seven are Lights, Recognition, Badge, Tools, Instruction, Name, and Return.

These fourteen acts must be done in sequence as required by Masonic Law, Masonic Information, and Strict Examination. Any missed, removed actions or watering down is considered an unworthy and ignorant initiation.

What does it say about the man who looks more at his watch than his duty, fails to prepare than to practice, chooses ignorance over intellect, or prefers the popular wrong over the ritualistic right?

Reflecting on my initiation, I remember going through so many emotions and anxieties. At that moment, I recall being told beforehand that it would be a beautiful and humbling experience.

Now, as a well-informed and worthy mason, which I have advanced into, I often playback in my mind my initiation as I went through all 14 acts. Back then, I was very impressed with my first masonic experience. However, as time passed, I realized how much was left out and watered down.

When I participated in my first initiation as a Master Mason and the many that have followed since I saw firsthand why we as a craft have lost the essence and beauty of the "Part" of The Hidden Mysteries; it comes down to a lack of proper planning, time, practice, and learning.

Hence, I have written this book to shed light and inspire many to go back or, in some cases, start searching for more light in masonry, as our covenant requires us to do of our own free will and accord.

Lectures:
Merriam-Webster Dictionary defines "Lectures" *as 1a - discourse given before an audience or class, especially for instruction;* **2:** *a formal reproof.*

Masonry defines *"**The Lectures**" as "Each Degree of Freemasonry contains a course of instruction, in which the ceremonies, traditions, and moral education appertaining to the Degree is set forth. This arrangement is called a Lecture.*

Each lecture, for convenience and to conform to certain divisions in the ceremonies, is divided into sections, the number of which has varied at different periods, although the substance remained the same. (Mackey's Encyclopedia, History of Freemasonry, and Macoy's Cyclopedia)

The EA° Lectures are composed of two parts and one section:

<u>The First Part</u> is dedicated entirely to a detailed walk-through of the initiation while summarizing and demonstrating the initiation ceremonies, including practicing the First Masonic Landmark.

<u>The Second Part</u> is a complete explanation of the ceremonies detailed in the first, the two together delivering the reasons for the *"why"* and *"wherefores"* of the ritualistic symbolism.

<u>The Third Section</u> is exclusively occupied with a detailed description of the significance of the fifteen symbols peculiar to this EA°.

The best lecturers involve teaching, mentoring, and leading by example. A practical and excellent way of illuminating others is incorporating props and illustrations such as Tracing Boards, didactic role-playing, and study halls.

In masonry, providing lecturers is a simple science when the lecturer is well prepared and proficient in his craft and has an open mind and heart to learn from his audience's interaction, as opposed to the chaos of being unprepared, unworthy, ignorant, and closed-minded to learning from others.

Reflecting on the Hidden Mysteries of Ancient Freemasonry (The Art, The Part, The Point)

The Point |

Merriam-Webster Dictionary defines "Point": *1a: an individual detail, 1b: the most important essential in a discussion or matter, an end or object to be achieved.*

Masonry defines *"The Point" of the Mysteries of Masonry as "The points referred to in the ritualistic phrase, arts, parts, and points of the hidden mysteries of Masonry" are the rules and regulations of the Institution- Phillips's New World of Words (1706 edition) defines point as "a head or chief matter." It is in this sense that we speak of the points of Freemasonry.*

A rather significant use of the word is where it means to correct and complete the openings left between the stones in a wall meaning applied by the operative craftsmen that are very old and still very apt to this day" (Mackey's Encyclopedia, History of Freemasonry, and Macoy's Cyclopedia)

The EA° ritualistic protocol and doctrine are governed by the Ritual, Constitution, Monitor, Edicts, and Prerogatives adopted by each jurisdiction. In addition, the Landmarks of Freemasonry can never be changed or altered. Since the Entered Apprentice degree is the foundation of all Masonry and the only degree that makes a man a mason, it should always be conducted in due and ancient form as our ancients intended.

Every mason is responsible and obligated to be well-versed, informed, and proficient in the Entered Apprentice Degree and Ritualistic Initiation.

Priority should always be given to practice as a team before every initiation or degree work. It is unworthy and ignorant <u>not</u> to be duly and truly prepared, worthy, and well qualified. There are better times to practice than just before or during the ritualistic work. Believing that the degree work can be done just by reading or winging it. To do so is un-masonic behavior.

This would be considered defrauding the lodge and the craft. In Masonry," say the ancient lectures, "twelve original points" form the root of the structure and understanding of the initiation ritual. Without ALL these points, no man was or can be, legally and essentially received into the fraternity.

Every man made a Mason must go through all these twelve forms and ceremonies, not only in the first degree but in every subsequent one. Respecting these points is of the highest importance in the fraternity's traditions; our ancient brethren exercised great ingenuity in giving them symbolic explanations and referring the twelve parts of the initiation ceremony to the twelve tribes of Israel.

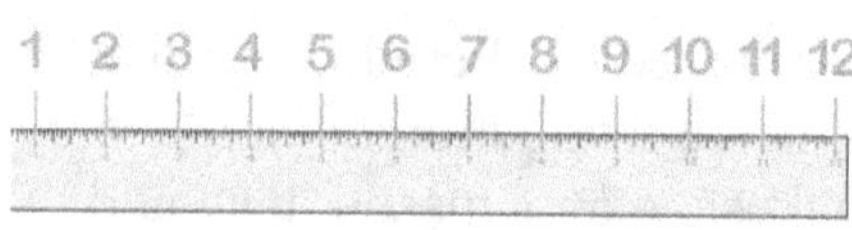

Notwithstanding the value and importance our ancient brethren deemed these points to possess, the Grand Lodge of England thought proper, at the Union in 1813, to strike the twelve points from its rituals and substitute three "new" points. Neither of these systems has ever been practiced in this country; the "four" perfect points" constitute an adequate substitute for both.

However, we can infer that the consolidation of the twelve tribes of Israel under four banners does explain the rationale behind going from twelve points to four points. It's unmistakable that it is still honoring and preserving the original twelve points into four.

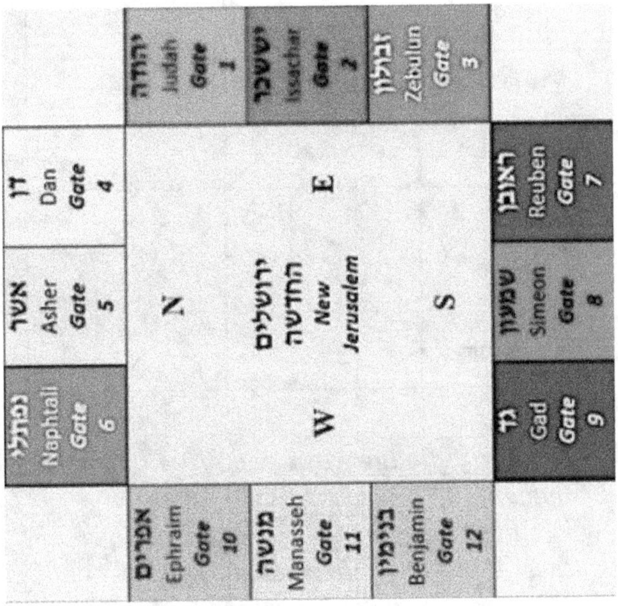

The symbolism embraced would then be broken down into four sections of three parts. Symbolically walking through the Israeli Camp as described in *Exodus 1:1-5, Revelation 7:5-8, Numbers 2:1-14, 3:38*

The Twelve Original Points

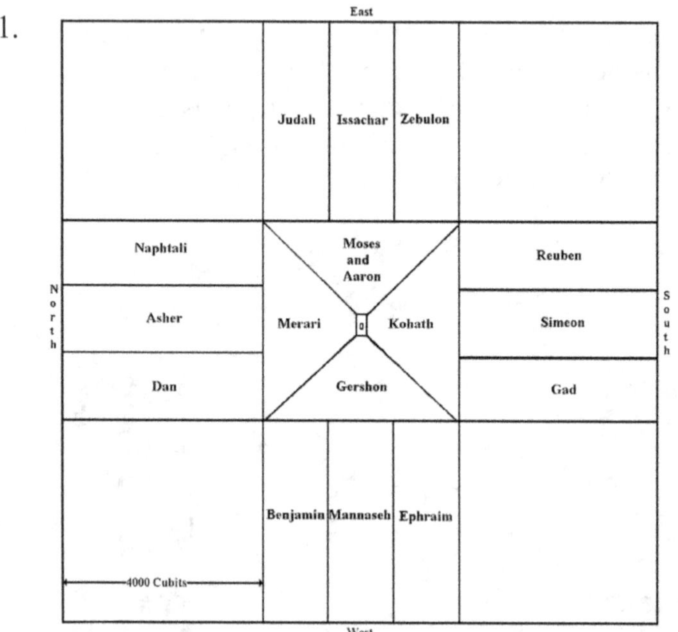

The opening of the Lodge *was symbolized by the tribe of Reuven (Reuben), because he was the firstborn of his father Jacob, who called him "the beginning of his strength," the door, as it were, by which the children of Israel entered the world. He was, therefore, appropriately adopted as the emblem of that ceremony, which is essentially the beginning of every initiation.* **BANNER Reuben**

2. **_The preparation of the candidate_** was symbolized by the tribe of Simeon because Simeon prepared the instruments for the slaughter of the Shechemites, which excited the heavy displeasure of his parent; therefore, to perpetuate abhorrence of his cruelty, candidates for initiation were deprived of all weapons, both offensive and defensive.

Remember from the scriptures that Shechem violated the chastity of Simeon's sister, Dinah, and his brother Levi killed the Shechemites during the third day of recovery from their circumcision. This is a period when the male organ is most sensitive when circumcised as an adult. **BANNER Reuben**

3. **_The report of the Senior Deacon_** referred to the tribe of Levi in commemoration of the signal or report that Levi was supposed to have given to his brother Simeon when they assailed the men of Shechem at a time when they were incapable of defending themselves, and put them all to the sword, because of the affront which, Dinah, their sister, had received from Shechem, the son of Hamor. **BANNER Dan and Reuben**

4. **_The entrance of the candidate_** into the Lodge was symbolized by the tribe of Judah because they were the first to cross the river Jordan and enter the promised land of "milk and honey," coming from the darkness and servitude, as it were, of the wilderness by many dangerous and wearisome journeys into the light and liberty of Canaan. **BANNER Juda**

5. ***The prayer was symbolized*** by Zevulun (Zebulun) because the blessing and prayer of Jacob were given to Zevulun in preference to his brother Issachar. **BANNER Juda**

6. ***The circumambulation*** referred to the tribe of Issachar because, as a thriftless and indolent tribe, they required a leader to advance them to an equal elevation with the other tribes. **BANNER Juda**

7. ***The advancing to the altar*** was symbolized by the tribe of Dan, that the candidate might be taught by contrast to advance in the way of truth and holiness as rapidly as this tribe advanced to idolatry, for it was among the tribe of Dan that the serpent was first set up for adoration. **BANNER Dan**

8. ***The obligation referred*** to the tribe of Gad in allusion to the solemn vow, which was made by Jephthah, Judge of Israel, who was of that tribe. **BANNER Reuben**

9. ***The entrusting of the candidate with the mysteries*** was symbolized by the tribe of Asher because he was then presented with the rich fruits of Masonic knowledge, as Asher was said to be the inheritor of fatness and royal dainties.
BANNER Dan

10. ***The investiture of the lambskin***, by which the candidate is declared free, referred to the tribe of Naphtali, which was invested by Moses with peculiar freedom, when he said, "O, Naphtali, satisfied with favor and fill with the blessing of the Lord, possess thou the West and the South."
BANNER Dan

11. ***The ceremony of the northeast corner*** of the Lodge referred to Joseph because as this ceremony reminds us of the most superficial part of Masonry, so the two half tribes of **Ephraim** and **Manasseh**, of which the tribe of Joseph was composed, were accounted to be more superficial than the rest, as they were the descendants of the grandsons only of Jacob. ***BANNER Ephraim***

12. ***The closing of the Lodge*** was symbolized by the tribe of Benjamin, the youngest of Jacob's sons, and thus closed his father's strength. ***BANNER Ephraim***

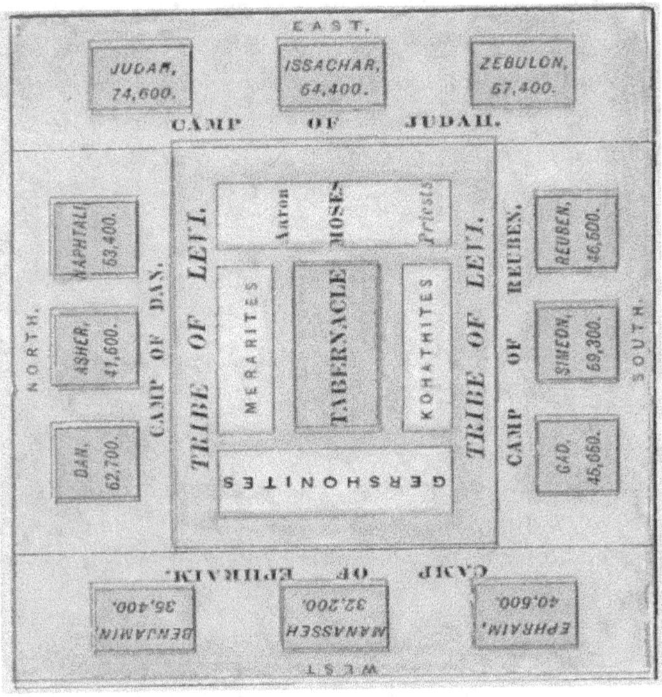

In the earliest lectures of the eighteenth century, these were called Principal Points. The designation of them as Perfect Points of Entrance was of a later date. They are described both in the English and the American systems.

Their specific names, and their allusion to the four cardinal virtues, are the same in both; but the verbal explanations differ, although not substantially. They are so-called because they refer to four essential points of the initiation.

*The **Guttural** refers to the entrance upon the penal responsibilities; the **Pectoral** to the entrance into the Lodge; the **Manual** to the entrance to the Covenant; and the **Pedal** to the entrance on the instructions in the northeast. (Mackey's Encyclopedia, History of Freemasonry, and Macoy's Cyclopedia)*

<u>The Cardinal Virtues</u>

*They are **temperance**, **fortitude**, **prudence**, and **justice**. They are referred to in the ritual of the Entered Apprentice Degree and will be found in this work under their respective heads.*

Oliver says (Revelations of a Square, chapter 1) that in the eighteenth century, the Freemasons delineated the symbols of the four cardinal virtues by an acute angle variously disposed.

Thus, suppose you face the east; the angle symbolizing temperance will point to the south. It was called a Guttural. Fortitude was denoted by a saltire or Saint Andrew's Cross, X. This was the Pectoral.

The symbol of prudence was an acute angle pointing toward the southeast and denominated a Manual; justice had its angle toward the north and was called a Pedestal or Pedal. The possession of cardinal virtues is no special distinction of Freemasons, for other societies have had them. (Mackey's Encyclopedia, History of Freemasonry, and Macoy's Cyclopedia)

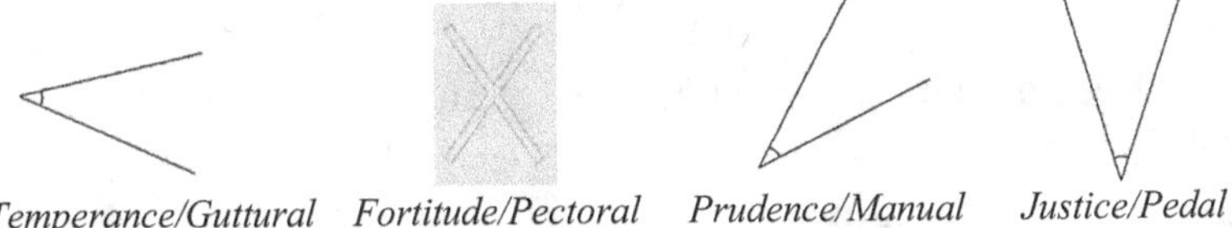

Temperance/Guttural   Fortitude/Pectoral   Prudence/Manual   Justice/Pedal

As I reflect on the perfect points of my entrance and the allusion to the four cardinal virtues, at first look, I did not see the connection or relationship as per the Masonic definition; this was way over my head.

However, I thought the definition of an acute angle *is "An angle measuring less than 90 degrees. That's why it's called an acute angle. This angle is smaller than the right angle (which is equal to 90 degrees). For example, $\angle 30^o$, $\angle 45^o$, $\angle 60^o$, $\angle 75^o$, etc. are all acute angles".* I was initially assuming they all had the same angle.

Now I am starting to see my true reflection. I recall my conductor referencing something about a point within a circle, and I represented the point within, and the circle represents the earth.

So, if our ancient brethren connected the Cardinal points of (*N, S, E, W)* to the Cardinal virtues *(F,T,P,J),* the key to all of this must be in plain sight.

How do I make sense of all of this? Are we talking about a circle and a square? How are they connected? So, what do they both have in common?

The first reflection I had; if I take a square and stretch it from west to east, the square becomes a rectangle. I remember something from the *Third Section Lecture* that references the shape of the lodge being a representation of the earth even though it was shaped as a rectangle.

Now we are getting somewhere. Two squares together make a rectangle, so if the Lodge represents the Earth, then half of the lodge will have sunlight shining on it, and the other will be dark (*12 am or 12 pm*).

So then one square would be represented by a white square and the other by a black square, hmm: interesting…. Then my second reflection was, what would I uncover if I used the same process as I did with the square but with a circle?

If I take a 360°circle and stretch it, it will now become an oval shape. Now this is getting very interesting. I recall my conductor telling me, *"To try to form somehow an angle of an oblong."*

Then it dawned on me how I circumambulated in the lodge. As the point within the circle and both the lodge and the circle represent the world or earth that, somehow, they are both the same. But is a Square and a Circle the same?

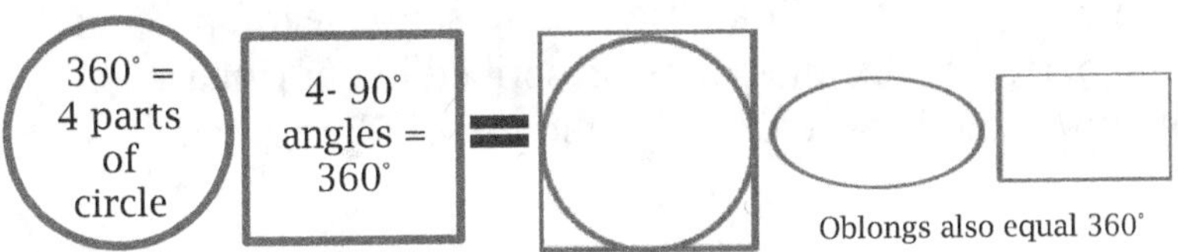

As I see these shapes and connect the Lectures, the initiation to the masonic definitions starts making sense.

The Cardinal Points is how we travel directionally on earth in a physical sense. The Cardinal Virtues is how we travel in a spiritual or behavioral sense.

Our ancient brethren connected acute angles to points and virtues using Ancient Mysteries. Since an acute angle is less than 90 degrees, this means that we can fit four acute angles in a Right Angle of 90 degrees or ¼ part of a circle.

I can fit acute angles at 30°, 45°, 60°, and 75°, hence the masonic definition. Each acute angle is 15°. Wait a minute; aren't these the same degrees on the true quadrant of a Past Master's jewel? I just had a thought; can this number 15 mean something else?

30°	*45°*	*60°*	*75°*
Temperance/Guttural	*Fortitude/Pectoral*	*Prudence/Manual*	*Justice/Pedal*

I cannot help but see that those acute angles look like compasses, each separated by 15°. I need to search and see if there is any place in the lodge where I can see the tools that can make a square and a circle with a point in the middle…

My final reflection on the Arts, Parts, and Points of the Entered Apprentice Initiation. As I reflect on how important and necessary it is for all brethren to study, learn, practice, and perform ALL the points prescribed in our rituals, monitors, and constitutions without excluding any points.

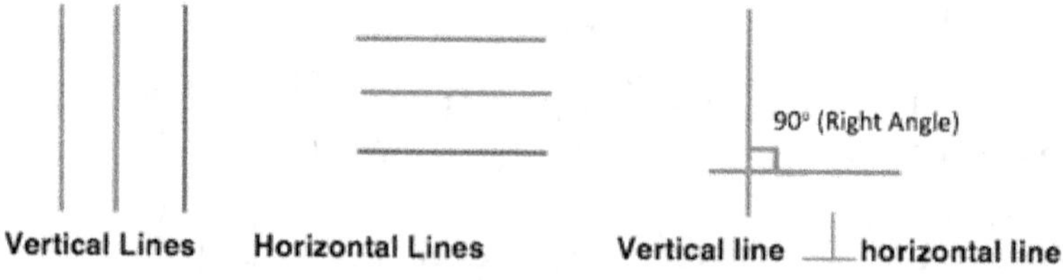

Vertical Lines   **Horizontal Lines**   **Vertical line**   **horizontal line**

Here is an example to consider; Let's take a 24-inch ruler, and we make a rule that each inch is emblematic of the hours of the day, hence 24 hours. Both the inches and hours represent all the required and necessary points for an Entered Apprentice candidate to be considered ritualistically initiated as a mason.

This means that the completion of the initiation must travel a full 24 inches or 24 hours. What does it say if we have to remove inches or hours because of a lack of studying, planning, practicing, and performance?

How can we travel 24 inches or 24 hours without disregarding our duties and responsibilities to the 24? And then choose to only travel 14 out of the 24 points? Are we our brother's keeper? Or are we initiating to a broken ruler or a broken clock?

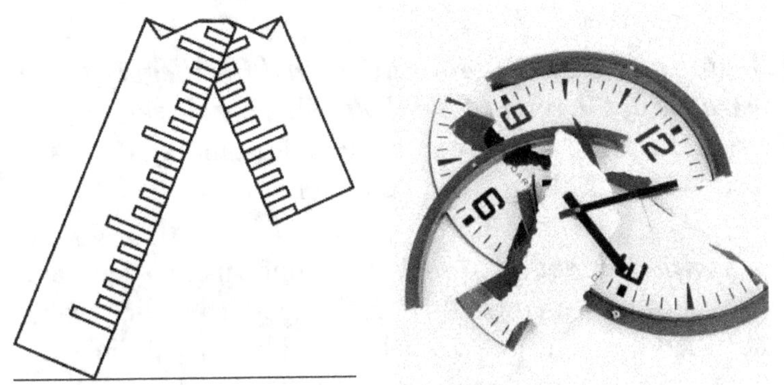

***Reflecting on the Three Lectures of**
**The Hidden Mysteries of Ancient Freemasonry
(Part One, Part Two, and Third Section)***

Part One (The Q. and A.)

According to the general acceptance of the term, Masonry is an art founded on the principles of Sacred Geometry and directed to the service and convenience of humanity. But freemasonry, embracing a more comprehensive range and having more nobler objectives in view, namely, the cultivation and improvement of the human mind, may with more propriety be called a science, in as much as availing itself of the terms of the former, it inculcates the principles of the purest morality. However, its lessons are, for the most part, veiled in allegory and illustrated by symbols. (*Hemming.*)

A Beautiful System Of Morality, Veiled In Allegory, Illustrated By Signs And Symbols. This is a direct form of Masonic rhetoric, and its complete understanding is embedded in the allegory of the Order.

A Beautiful System Of Morality: reminds us of The Grand Architect of the Universe's system, or pattern, which was established for us to follow each day of our lives. That system is The Grand Architect of the Universe's Moral Law. These Laws are segmented into ten primary instructions known as The Ten Commandments.

Veiled in Allegory: reminds us that the Hidden Mysteries of Freemasonry can only be found and understood when we search *(read)* our rituals, monitors, dictionaries, and Volume of Sacred Law for greater depth and understanding in those things deemed secretive in Masonry.

Illustrated By Signs And Symbols: verifies the fact that Masonry is hidden and that it is secretive. Like the symbols we display openly, our signs, words, grips, characters, etc., carry a definite surface meaning. Yet, we find spiritual, material, physical, and intellectual allegories below that surface.

If, in the Lodge, we remove all signs, words, grips, and *hieroglyphics* (symbols and characters), what remains is the craft and The Grand Architect of the Universe's gift to humanity, which is the Volume of Sacred Law. Still, we have not moved Masonry; only the illustrations and projection modes have been moved.

The allegories of Masonry are still present in the Volume of Sacred Law. This is to say that Masonry is no more, and no less, than the study of man and practice of all religions, spirituality, and Sacred Sciences, and the guiding of our actions within the realm of The Grand Architect of the Universe's Law. (*Mackey's Encyclopedia, History of Freemasonry, Macoy's Cyclopedia & Dictionary of Freemasonry, and Albert Pike's Morals and Dogmas*)

Reflecting on the passages above, I can see how sciences, spirituality, and intellectual growth and development are becoming the main common factors as I evolved as an Entered Apprentice.

Learning the principles of morality and behavior with purpose, guidance, and direction can be overwhelming at this stage as an Entered Apprentice.

As I think about evolving and growing the Intellect and spiritual essence of man through a system of morality veiled in allegory and illustrated by signs and symbols.

 I realized there is a specific pattern and sequence connected and interlaced within words and how they are being instructed through grammar and rhetoric while challenging the logic that I must process in making sense of these new sciences and behaviors I am being taught at this stage.

Reflecting on the Three Lectures of
The Hidden Mysteries of Ancient Freemasonry
(Part One, Part Two, and Third Section)

One observation that mainly contributed to the sense that I felt as an Entered Apprentice was that going through much information in a short period made me feel lost and overwhelmed.

As I reflect, I realize that it was not about the quantity of the information but about the language that felt Shakespearian and biblical.

Many words I had never seen before. For those I did know, I soon learned that all these words I struggled with had multiple meanings and depended on the context in which they were being used.

I spoke with my conductor and expressed how I felt; I may have made a mistake. For privacy and respect, I will refer to my conductor as Bro. Vicious and his cable tow Bro. BvBABanker. Bro. Vicious started smiling and told me you have learned more than you think you know.

He then gave some of the best pieces of advice I have ever received as a mason; he told me, first, *"Question everything you know and always assume when dealing with masonic information that all the information it's hidden in plain sight within words, gestures, pictures, math, biblical verses, and stories.*

Secondly, be a detective; pay close attention to everything; **Details Matter***; follow what you think are clues and ask questions, not for the sake of seeking another man's version of his truth; but desire to find your truth with honesty and integrity and let your light shine the brightest". While always remembering that details matter. CJPJR (R.I.P.)*

After that conversation, I had mixed feelings; I understood what he was saying; however, it was easier said than done. I recall having a similar discussion with Bro. BvBABanker, what stuck with me the most was when he asked me what I thought about the first question in The First Part Lecture, also known as the Q and A.

(Side Note: I understand different jurisdictions use different Rituals, but for the most part, they are closely similar.)

In our Jurisdiction, the first question is "Whence Came you?" and the second question is "What came you here to do?' both questions, on the surface, are simple questions until I came across what both answers were. The first answer is "From the Holy Saints Johns of Jerusalem," and the second is "Learn to subdue my passion and improve myself in masonry."

My first reflections were what the heck? What does this even mean? Who speaks like this? I have never been to the Holy Saints Johns of Jerusalem; how can I subdue my passions and improve myself in masonry when I don't even know masonry? This is now going way over my head.

At this stage, I had to go back to what I had been taught and what I remember of my initiation. I decided to look at masonry as a puzzle; I had the pieces just needed to organize them.

I then remembered that I used to do many puzzles with my mother as a child. She taught me that when putting a puzzle together, first flip all pieces facing up, then organize all the edged pieces on one side and then all like color pieces on the other.

Finally, look at the box as a guide and map to find how each piece fell into place, and remember that the destination was not about organizing; it was about completing the puzzle.

My initial reflection on the first question, "Whence came you?" seemed trivial. Why, out of all the possible questions, is this one the first? Then I went back to the Arts, Parts, and Points of my initiation. The journey from the darkness of ignorance and unworthiness to the light of worthy intellectual knowledge and wisdom, spiritual and moral behaviors.

Now things are getting very interesting, "Whence came you?' had three different but collective interpretations. Using right angles, horizontals, and perpendiculars as a guide, I realized that this was a method of breaking the veils and allegories down to my truth or my light. So, I went into detective mode.

To be a good detective and wanting to use right angles, horizontals, and perpendiculars, I must first define the different contexts words have grammatically, along with the profane and the masonic definitions.

<u>Merriam-Webster Dictionary</u> defines "Right- Angles": *the angle bounded by two lines perpendicular to each other: an angle of 90° or ½ π radians.*

<u>Merriam-Webster Dictionary</u> defines "Horizontals": *1a: of or relating to the apparent junction of earth and sky: situated near the horizon b parallel to, in the plane of, or operating in a plane parallel to the horizon or baseline: the LEVEL horizontal distance a horizontal engine. 2: relating to, directed toward, or consisting of individuals or entities of similar status or on the same level: relating to or being transmission (as of a disease) by physical contact or proximity in contrast with inheritance*

"Perpendiculars": *1a: standing at right angles to the plane of the horizon: exactly upright b: being at right angles to a given line or plane. 2 extremely steep: PRECIPITOUS 3 of or relating to a medieval English Gothic style of architecture in which vertical lines predominate 4: relating to, uniting, or consisting of individuals of different types or on different levels.*

<u>Masonry defines</u> "Right Angles" *of the Mysteries of Masonry "A right angle is the meeting of two lines in an angle of ninety degrees or the fourth part of a circle. Each of its lines is perpendicular to the other, and as the perpendicular line is a symbol of uprightness of conduct, the right angle has been adopted by Masons as an emblem of virtue."*

<u>Masonry defines</u> *"Horizontals "or Plumb/Line. It is worthy of notice that, in most languages, the word used directly to indicate straightness of course or perpendicularity of position is also employed figuratively to express uprightness of conduct. Such is the Latin "rectum," which signifies at the same time a right line and honesty or integrity.*

<u>Masonry defines</u> *"Perpendiculars" In a geometrical sense, that which is upright and erect, leaning neither one way nor another. In a figurative and symbolic sense, it conveys the signification of Justice, Fortitude, Prudence, and Temperance. Justice that leans to no side but that of Truth. Fortitude, that yields to no adverse attack; Prudence, that ever pursues the straight path of integrity; and Temperance, that swerves not for appetite nor passion.*

Now looking at "Whence came You?" armed with the knowledge and meanings from a right-angle point of view was about "horizontal movements and perpendicular directions. This question is about where I was regarding my Intellectuality, Spirituality, and Morality.

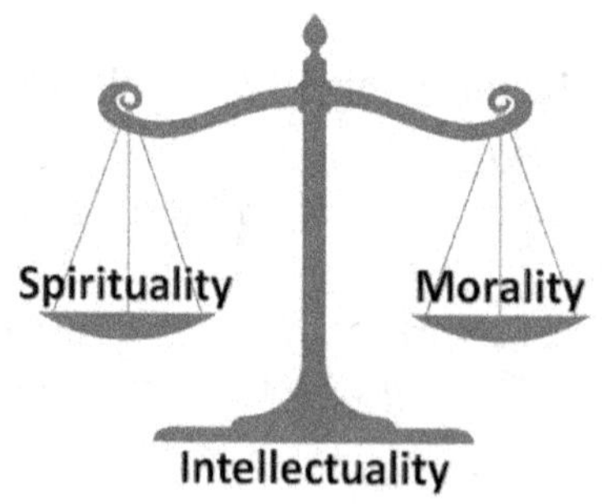

What shortfalls must I improve, and what abilities could I build on or strengthen? If I used a scale from 1-10 before masonry, I would rate my Intellect as about a 5, my spirituality as about a 4, and my morals about a 6.

"You Can't Really Know Where You Are Going Until You Know Where You Have Been" - **Maya Angelou.**

"If you do not know where you come from, then you don't know where you are, and if you don't know where you are, then you don't know where you're going. And if you don't know where you're going, you're probably going wrong."
– **Sir Terry Pratchett.**

"Whence came you?" meant I had recognized that I had many shortfalls and imperfections, just like a stone from the quarry that was not smooth, shaped, or polished. In fact, very rough, unshaped, and unpolished. So, how do I fix myself? Where do I go to improve me? Can I even fix myself?

These are all thoughts from darkness in the sense that I could not shed light on how to improve, evolve, strengthen, better, or gain wisdom or knowledge on my own.

In reflecting further on "Whence came you?" I realized that it had to be the first question. How can I start a journey if I do not know my starting point? This question was specific to where I came from an intellectual, spiritual, and moral viewpoint. Now this question makes so much sense to me.

The answer to the question "From the Lodge of the Holy Saints Johns of Jerusalem" at this stage still does not make as much sense to me or is as clear as the question is now. So, let us go back into detective mode.

Encyclopedia Britannica *"**St. John the Baptist,**" (born 1st decade BCE, Judaea, Palestine, near Jerusalem—died 28–36 CE; feast day June 24), Jewish prophet of priestly origin who preached the imminence of The Grand Architect of the Universe's Final Judgment and baptized those who repented in self-preparation for it; that he is revered among the Christian church as the forerunner of Jesus Christ.*

After a period of desert solitude, John the Baptist emerged as a prophet in the region of the lower Jordan River valley. He had a circle of disciples, and Jesus was among the recipients of his rite of baptism.

Encyclopedia Britannica *"**St. John the Evangelist**" one of the Twelve Apostles of Jesus and traditionally believed to be the author of the three Letters of John, the Fourth Gospel, and possibly the Revelation to John in the New Testament. He played a leading role in the early church in Jerusalem.*

<u>Merriam-Webster Dictionary</u> defines "Baptism" *1 **a***: *a Christian sacrament marked by ritual use of water and admitting the recipient to the Christian community **b***: *a non-Christian rite using water for ritual purification c Christian Science: purification by or submergence in Spirit **2***: *an act, experience, or ordeal by which one is purified, sanctified, initiated, or named.*

<u>Merriam-Webster Dictionary</u> defines "Evangelist." *1 often capitalized a writer of any of the four Gospels **2***: *a person who evangelizes specifically: a Protestant minister or layman who preaches at special services **3***: *an enthusiastic advocate.*

<u>Masonry defines</u> *"**St. John the Baptist**" in the Mysteries of Masonry. He was the forerunner of Jesus, a son of the Jewish priest Zacharias and of Elizabeth, who, as a zealous judge of morality and undaunted preacher of repentance, obtained great celebrity, first in his native country, then in the mountains of Judea, and afterward among the whole nation.*

His simple and self-disciplined manner of living contributed much to his fame, especially the peculiar purification or consecration by a baptism in a river bath, which he introduced as a symbol of that moral purity that he so zealously inculcated Mastery in. (MaCoys's Cyclopedia)

<u>Masonry defines</u> *"**St. John the Evangelist**." St. John, the Evangelist, and Apostle of · Jesus, whose gospel is so vital to all Freemasons, was born in Bethsaida, in Gidilee, a son of Zebedee, and a disciple of Jesus, who Loved him because he distinguished himself by his gentleness and humility.*

He was a man of great energy and poetic fire and lite, in his early years somewhat haughty and intolerant, but afterward an example of love. (MaCoys's Cyclopedia)

<u>Merriam-Webster Dictionary</u> defines "Veiled." ***1 a****: having or wearing a veil or a concealing cover a veiled hat* ***b****: characterized by a softening tonal distortion* ***2****: obscured as if by a veil: DISGUISED.*

<u>Merriam-Webster Dictionary</u> defines "Allegories" ***1****: the expression by means of symbolic fictional figures and actions of truths or generalizations about human existence. A writer is known for fusing allegory also: an instance (as in a story or painting) of such expression. The poem is an allegory of love and jealousy.* ***2****: a symbolic representation.*

<u>Masonry defines</u> *"**Allegory**" as A discourse or narrative in which there is a literal and a figurative sense, a patent, and a connected meaning; the literal or patent sense being intended, by analogy or comparison, to indicate the figurative or concealed one.*

Its derivation from the Greek, "aUog and ayopeiv," to say something different, that is, to say something where the language is one thing and the true meaning another, exactly expresses the character of an allegory. (continue)

As I reflect on the first question and answer, Q- Whence came you? A- from the Lodge of the Holy Saint Johns of Jerusalem. Armed with all these definitions and multiple meanings of some common and not-so-common words and the work in researching them. I see the veil lifted and the allegories revealed from this simple Q and A.

Even though in language, it is asking, "Whence came you?" It is not literal as to where you are currently coming from. From the Lodge of the Holy Saint Johns is talking about something other than an actual building or geographical, physical location.

The Q and A are explicitly asking about where you are intellectually, spiritually, and morally before being initiated and where you are after the initiation.

The reference to the Holy Saint Johns is about how they portrayed and represented themselves as examples of morality, spirituality, and intellectual conduct. They set standards for others to follow in Jerusalem to the extent of one becoming a Grand Master.

Thus, the answer of "From a Lodge of the holy Saints John of Jerusalem" and armed with all these tools and sciences in the EA degree, my complete reflection of the first answer translates to me, "From a place of perfection favored of The Grand Architect of the Universe." Which is an allegorical narrative of man's experience in the Garden of Eden.

A place of perfection, favored by The Grand Architect of the Universe, where man could enjoy the warmth and knowledge of the Light of The Grand Architect of the Universe.

The second question:
Q-"What came you here to do?"
A- "Learn to subdue my passions and improve myself in masonry."

My initial reflection on Q-"What came you here to do?" is an excellent follow-up to the first question, but what is it alluding to? or what is the meaning? Since I know this question is veiled in allegory and illustrated by signs and symbols, there must be an exoteric and esoteric design behind it.

Knowing what I have learned, I must go back into detective mode to understand these questions in "Part One Lecture," it's time to put in the work! Let's detect…

<u>Merriam-Webster Dictionary</u> defines "Passion.*"1 a: the sufferings of Christ between the night of the Last Supper and his death. 2: the state or capacity of being acted on by external agents or forces. 3: the emotions as distinguished from reason. 4: intense, driving, or overmastering feeling or conviction. 5: an outbreak of anger. 6: a strong liking or desire for or devotion to some activity, object, or concept.*

<u>Merriam-Webster Dictionary</u> *defines "Improve." a: to enhance in value or quality : make better. b: to increase the value of (land or property) by making it more useful for humans (as by cultivation or the erection of buildings). 2: to use to good purpose.*

<u>Masonry defines</u> **"Passion"** of the Mysteries of Masonry *"The end, the moral, and purport of Masonry, is to subdue our passions; not to do our own will; to make daily progress in a laudable art; to promote morality, charity, good-fellowship, good nature, and humanity." (MaCoys' Cyclopedia)*

As I reflect on the Q- 'What came you here to do?' I must return to "whence I came"; my answer is to build and grow true acceptance and intellectual honesty, conversing philosophies between men.

The need to understand and develop consideration in the individual condition, the need for me to grow not only as a good citizen of our own country like the EA charge states, but a genuine and trustworthy brother in all of The Grand Architect of the Universe's world.

More so, "What came you here to do?" This question aims to our purpose as masons in our personal actions and among each other. Additionally, what is my priority when spending time in the Lodge? What is my purpose when in an EA Lodge or study hall? What specifically am I looking for? What am I here for?

These are all sub-questions that I may have yet to have all the answers to at this stage in masonry. Why do men become masons? Or why did I become a Mason?

One of the first primary directions as individuals as we progress in our lives as men and Masons is to improve our Masonic Education continuously.

I came here to learn; the ritual demonstrates that we are to initiate an ongoing learning journey and apply these lessons to our daily lives. Through this process, we improve ourselves as men and Masons. In a masonic sense, we start as a rough ashlar.

<u>Merriam-Webster Dictionary</u> *defines* <u>**"Rough"**</u> *1a: marked by inequalities, ridges, or projections on the surface.* <u>**"Ashlar"**</u> *1: hewn or squared stone also: masonry of such stone. **2***: a thin, squared, and dressed stone for facing a wall of rubble or brick.*

An uneven and incomplete piece of work has potential but could be of better use in its current form. As we grow and evolve intellectually, spiritually, and morally in Freemasonry, we should always benefit from the lessons taught.

As EAs, we are given specific tools to assist and aid us in the journey. We now shift our attention away from the vices and superfluities of life to focus on those intellectual, spiritual, and moral elements that are the makings of life truly rewarding.

As we progress on becoming a finished stone, striving to be that perfect ashlar and become useful to the Great Architect of the Universe's purpose and use.

As I reflect on the A- "Learn to subdue my passions and improve myself in masonry." I come across words and some I have never used or seen before, such as "Superfluities."

<u>Merriam-Webster Dictionary</u> defines "Superfluities" *1a: EXCESS, OVERSUPPLY **b**: something unnecessary or superfluous. 2: immoderate and especially luxurious living, habits, or desires.*

The next component of our purpose is "to subdue our passions." These passions are the crude and base characteristics of all men that can separate us from the civilized company of others and lead to destructive results.

Greed, impatience, pride, jealousy, and lust are just some of those superfluities that serve the uncivilized qualities of a man and lead to divisions between us, interfering with our ability to cooperate, collaborate, and benefit from uniting our mutual talents and efforts. They prevent us from pursuing more admirable goals and accomplishing great things for the benefit of all.

As we pursue our improvement, enjoyment, and standing above those around us for selfish reasons, we do so at the expense of others. We are told that subduing our passions is a worthy destination to be actively always pursued by all Masons. Temperance, one of our cardinal virtues, cautions us to avoid the excesses that render man weak.

With this warning, we are given the responsibility of learning to keep our desires within due bounds to avoid them interfering with everyday and practical thoughts. We are providing the **Compasses**, one of our great lights, to assist us with this task.

This helpful tool has one particular function: defining the circle around the point that defines to subdue my passions" means that through the true teachings of Masonry, one learns to bring commanding and overpowering emotions and desires under control.

As I take all this in, I realize that as I progress through the Entered Apprentice degree and all those I pursue after. I must learn the Rituals and then work on solving, defining, and researching beyond the language.

Look for those clues; see this as a detective would lift veils and reveal the true allegories. I will not go further into the Q and A beyond the first two.

My goal is to give an example of how to define, research, and travel through the masonic allegories, signs, and symbols and share a process that will allow all Entered Apprentices to find their truth and shine their light the brightest.

Reflecting on the Three Lectures of The Hidden Mysteries of Ancient Freemasonry (Part One, Part Two, and Third Section)

Part Two ("Why" and "Wherefores")

The "Part Two Lecture," also known as the "Why" and "Wherefores," is an actual account and detailed explanation of the Arts, Parts, and Points of the Entered Apprentice Degree.

The second section of the first lecture, or "Part Two," according to the system mainly used in this country, is engaging with a description of the symbolic meaning of the art, parts, and points that are detailed in "Part One"; without, knowledge of the second section, the first becomes unfruitful and unimportant.

It must, however, be acknowledged that many of the interpretations given in this section are insufficient to the developed mind and seem to have been accepted on the belief of the old Egyptians, who used symbols to conceal rather than express their thoughts.

Studied (*worthy*) Masons have always been determined to go beyond the lectures' mere details and stereotyped phrases.

Looking at the history and the philosophy of the ancient religions and the organization of the ancient mysteries for a true explanation of most of the symbols of Masonry, and there among the symbols, they have always been enabled to find this true interpretation.

These lectures are, however, still preserved as a brief method of gaining general knowledge of the mode of Masonic instruction and as providing appropriate proof of the definition that *"**Freemasonry is a system of morality veiled in allegory and illustrated by signs and symbols.**"*

As I reflect on "Part Two" and as I go through the ritual, I also go back in my mind and playback my Initiation and start connecting those movements and actions with the definitions of "why" and "wherefore."

This is the first moment as an EA that I start to see and have the foundation of the Ancient Mysteries unveiled and revealed alongside an initial understanding of what " Illustrated by signs and symbols" means.

As I explained earlier, there are two parts to the Entered Apprentice Initiation and 14 acts divided into two sections. One section has seven acts while in darkness (hoodwink) and seven acts while being illuminated or seeing the light.

The Fourteen Acts Illustrated by Signs and Symbols:
*Preparation, Alarm, Received, Invoking, Traveling, Stations,
Covenant, Lights, Recognition, Badge, Tools, Instruction,
Name, and Return.*

Tracing Boards from The Manual of the Lodge. 1862

50

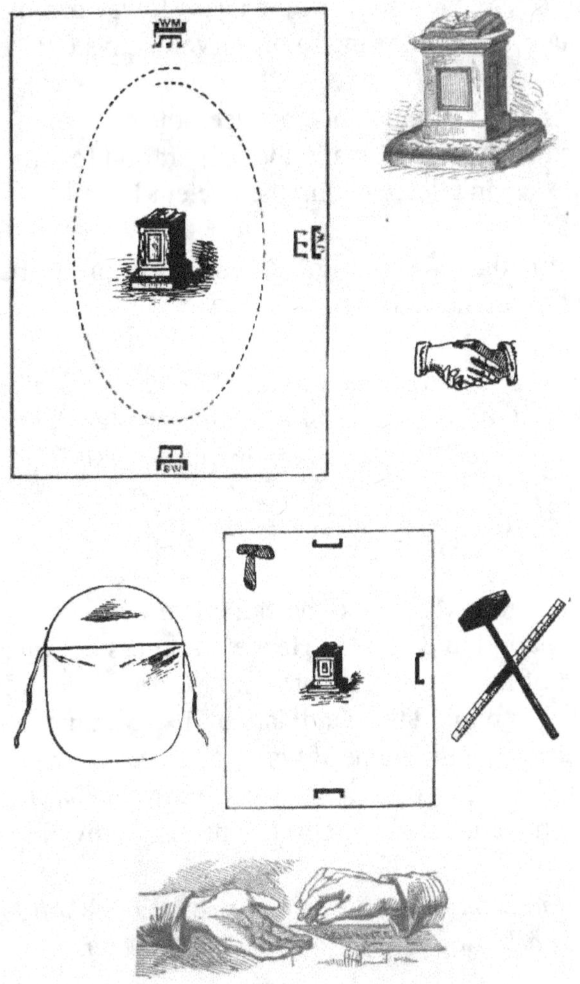

Tracing Boards from The Manual of the Lodge. 1862

51

I want to reflect on some of the acts. However, I must stay cautious while still trying to preserve its mystery.

There is much resemblance between the candidate's preparation in Masonry and the preparation for entering the Temple, as practiced among the ancient Israelites.

The Talmudical thesis entitled "*Beracoth*" prescribes the regulation in these words:

" No man shall enter into the Lord's house with his staff (an offensive weapon), nor with his outer garment, nor with shoes on his feet, nor with money in his purse. "

Preparation:

In the Ancient Mysteries, the candidate was always kept for a certain period in darkness. Hence, darkness became the symbol of initiation. Applicable to Masonic symbolism, it is intended to remind the candidate of his ignorance, which Masonry is to enlighten; of his evil nature, which Masonry is to purify; of the world, in whose shadows he has been wandering, and from which Masonry is to unveil to him.

"Ask, and it shall be given you; seek, and ye shall find; knock, and it shall be opened unto you. -Matthew vii. 7. "

Invoking:

As Masons, we are taught never to initiate any great or significant undertaking without first invoking the blessing and protection of the Grand Architect of the Universe. This is because Masonry is a spiritual institution, not **a religious organization or religion**, and we thereby show our dependence on our trust in The Grand Architect of the Universe.

Recognition:

The Right hand has in all ages been deemed an emblem of fidelity, and our ancient brethren worshiped Deity under the name of Fides or Fidelity, which was sometimes represented by two right hands, joined, and sometimes by two human figures, holding each other by the right hands.

Instructions:

THE LESSON OF CHARITY.
Although Freemasonry is indebted for its origin to its
religious and philosophic integrity, masonry has adapted to
the relief of the distressed, a significant feature in its
teachings. Hence it has been well said that there is no
institution whose laws are more strongly enforced or whose
teachings more deeply inculcate the virtue of charity.

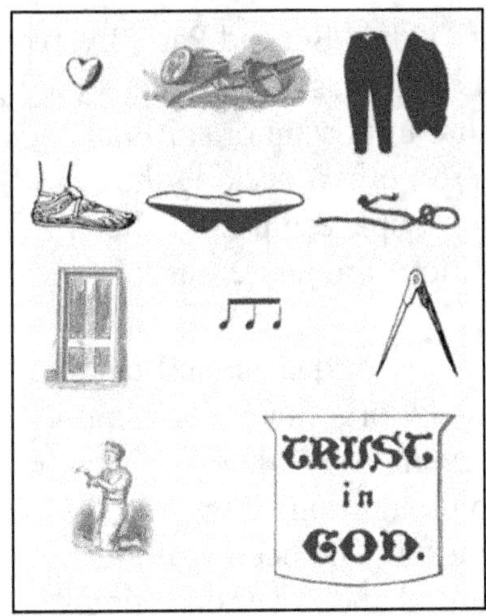
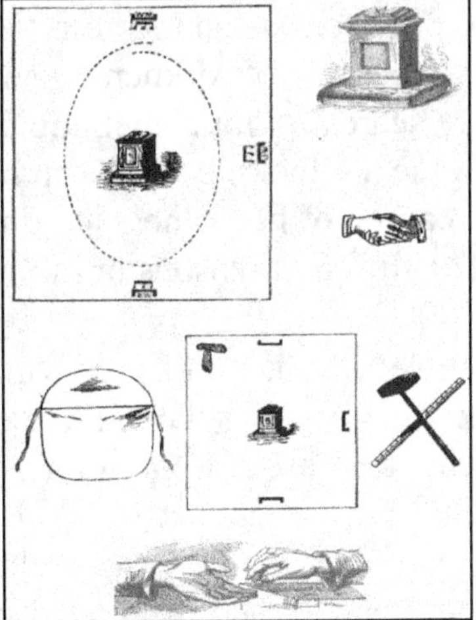

As I reflected on these two illustrations at first glance, when first introduced early in the Entered Apprentice degree, I must admit it wasn't very clear. However, when I received the "First Part Lecture," I was first exposed to this, still a little confusing at this stage of the Entered Apprentice Degree.

Subsequently, when I received the "Second Part Lecture," is when it all made sense. Each was explained in detail and sequence as my conductor connected the twelve points and the fourteen acts of the initiation. I was impressed with how the "in darkness' and "in light" came together to form an eclipse or the joining of a horizontal and a perpendicular.

My reflections on the "First Part" and "Second Part" Lectures
are mixed. Lots of men come to Freemasonry. Perhaps they
are searching for something more important or spiritual.
Some are looking for conspiracies, others seeking the
meaning of life, others looking for spaceships and aliens...
The different reasons or motivations are numerous.

However, when I engage with many of these men I come
across, it always works; like clockwork, many don't know
what they are searching for or even know what they want to
find. I can relate because I also thought one thing and found
much more than I was searching for. The beauty of the
journey continues to blow my mind and never disappoints.

In a sense, the passage "<u>blindfolded</u> and <u>groping</u> around in
the dark." For me hit home because I felt blindfolded trying
to learn something different and spiritual at that stage; I did
not realize that it would take time to read, research, and
practice.

These two circumstances are represented in the two sections
of the First-Degree Ritual: one of groping ignorantly in the
dark for the Truth behind our earthly existence; and one of
discovering light with the opened eyes of the Initiate.

Freemasonry requires that every Candidate for Initiation
comes "properly prepared." What does that mean? It answers
the question: "Where were you first prepared to be a
Mason?" The answer, as you know, is "in your heart."

Every ancient and modern Initiates system has required this as a prerequisite. Only then can an Initiation be meaningful because it is meant to create a psychological change in the interested candidate, which leads to a new outlook: of humility, realizing that one has been in the dark; of eagerness, for seeking and receiving light; of hope: for spiritual enlightenment.

***Reflecting on the Three Lectures of**
***The Hidden Mysteries of Ancient Freemasonry**
(Part One, Part Two, and Third Section)*

Third Section

*The third section of the Entered Apprentice's lecture explains
the nature and principles of our constitution, and furnishes
many interesting details relating to the Form, Supports,
Covering, Furniture, Ornaments, Lights, and Jewels of a
Lodge, how it should be situated, and to whom dedicated.
Nearly the whole of this section has been made monitorial.*

*Webb, and after him, Cross, Hardie, Tannehill, and all other
monitorial writers, have left but little of it unpublished. I
have, on the same principle, slightly increased the amount of
information given by the publication of one or two passages
hitherto excepted from publication in other monitors since I
could discover no reason why this exception should have
been made.* **(Albert Mackey)**

As I reflect on the "Third Section," I learned that this section
is about understanding the "Whys" and "Wherefores" of
initial masonic protocol and structure and how they are
connected.

As I learned the fifteen lessons, I could not help but see the
pattern and connections with the physical and spiritual steps
leading me to understand Masonic intellect and moral
doctrine better.

In other words, it was at this stage that I understood the knowledge thus far and how it was increasing my spiritual and moral wisdom of the ancient mysteries.

As I participated in my Entered Apprentice Lodge proceedings, I found the lecture information more meaningful and illuminating.

My conductor for study hall would have us role-play the didactic open and close of the Entered Apprentice degree. It indeed was a fantastic experience for us.

As I replay all the different teaching methods that my conductor used, the didactic role-playing opened my mind and heart to see, hear, and feel the true knowledge and wisdom of the Ancient Mysteries.

Think about this for a second. Imagine all the work and time to read, memorize, recite, and find purpose and understanding.

Then, to act it out and see all the allegories, signs, and symbols was mind-blowing for us. Then connecting and realizing I knew most of this information from being a man, free born, of lawful masonic age, and well recommended. It indeed was beautiful!

EUROPE
ASIA
MEDITERRANEAN
AFRICA
W   S   B

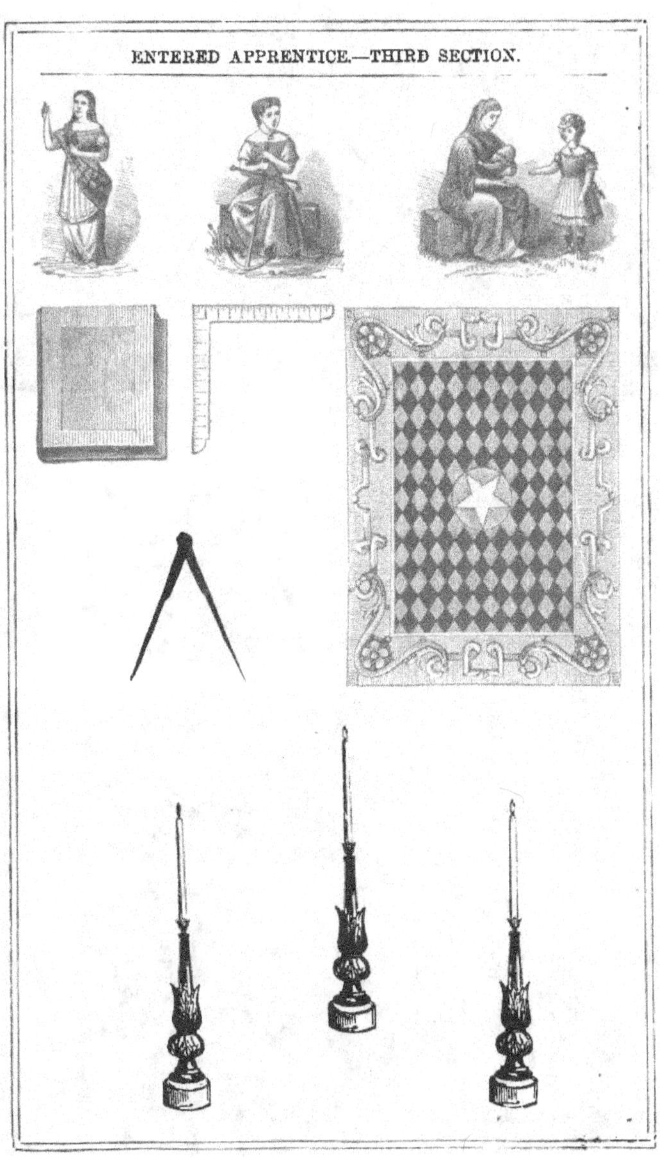

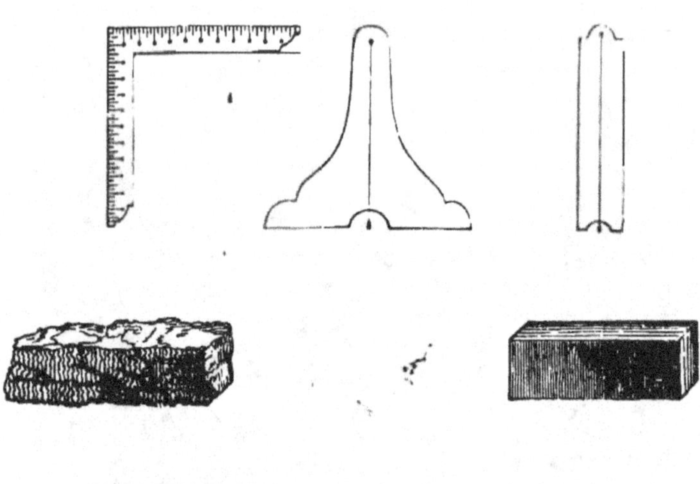

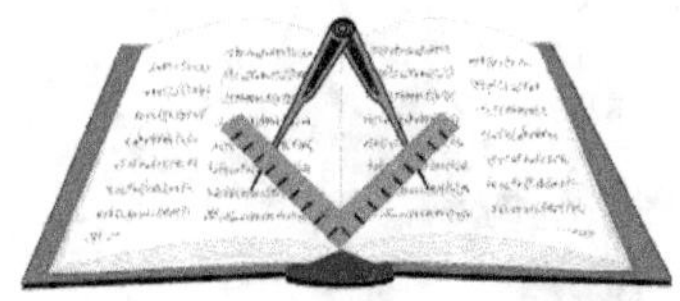 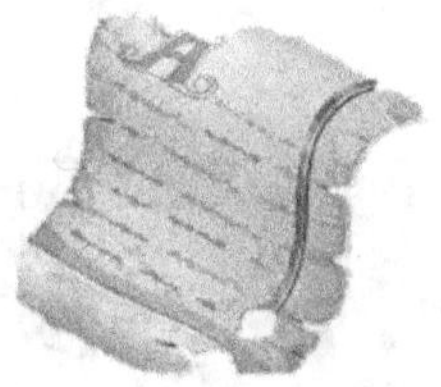

1- Lodge and 2- Charter

It is a gathering of Masons duly assembled, having the Holy Bible, Square, and Compasses, and a Charter or Warrant of Constitution authorizing them to work.

Every lawful gathering of Masons, legally gathered for work, is called "a just and duly constituted Lodge." It is ***just***, *regular,* and *orderly* when it contains the requisite number to form a quorum and when the Bible, Square, and Compasses are present.

It is ***duly and legally constituted*** when acting under the authority of a Warrant of the Constitution, an instrument written and printed on parchment or paper (but appropriately, it should be on the former).

Originating from the Grand Lodge in whose jurisdiction the Lodge is located, and signed by the grand officers, which authorizes the persons therein named, and their successors, to meet as Masons and perform Masonic labor.

As no assembly of Masons is legal without such an instrument, it is not only the privilege but the duty of every Mason on his first visit to a strange Lodge to ask sight of its Warrant of Constitution; nor should any brother sit in a Lodge whose members are unwilling to exhibit the authority on which they act.

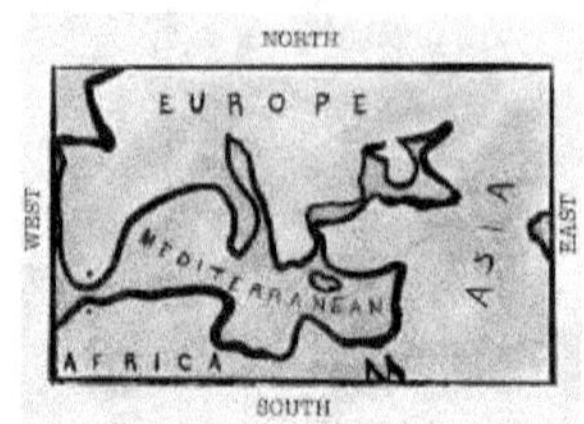

3- Held and 4- Form

Our ancient brethren met on the highest hills and in the lowest valleys, the better to observe the approach of cowans and eavesdroppers and to guard against surprise.

The reason assigned in the lecture for this assembling in high places is modern but not confirmed. The fact is that mountains and other high places were almost always considered holy and peculiarly appropriate for religious purposes.

We have abundant evidence in Scripture that the Jews were accustomed to worship on the tops of the highest hills, as it was believed that sacrifices offered from these elevated places were most acceptable to the Deity.

It was said that "the highest hills and the lowest valleys were, from the earliest times, deemed sacred, and it was supposed that the Spirit of God was peculiarly lingering in those places."

A Lodge is said, symbolically, to extend in length from east to west; in breadth, from north to south; in height, from the earth to the highest heavens; in-depth, from the surface to the center.

And a Lodge is said to be of these vast dimensions to denote the universality of Masonry and to teach us that Mason's charity should be equally as extensive.

5- Supports

A Lodge has three principal supports: Wisdom, *Strength*, and *Beauty* because there must be wisdom to contrive, strength to support, and beauty to adorn all significant undertakings.

Of these, the column of Wisdom is situated in the east part of the Lodge and is represented by the W∴ M∴ because it is presumed that he has the wisdom to devise labor for the craft, and to superintend them during the hours thereof.

The column of Strength is situated in the western part of the Lodge and is represented by the S∴ W∴ because it is his duty to strengthen and support the authority of this Master.

The column of Beauty is situated in the south part of the Lodge. It is represented by the J∴ W∴ because, from his position in the S,∴ he is the first to observe the meridian sun, which is the beauty and glory of the day, to call the craft from labor to refreshment, to superintend them during the hours thereof.

To see that none convert the purposes of refreshment into those of intemperance or excess, and to call them on again in due season, that the M∴ W∴ may have honor, and they pleasure and profit thereby.

The idea that the Lodge symbolizes the world is still being carried out. It was the belief of the ancients that the heavens, on the roof of the world, were supported by pillars.

Some suppose that the mountains are alluded to by these pillars but about a passage in Job xxvi. 11, where it is said, "The pillars of heaven tremble." Noyes thinks that "heaven is more probable to be represented as an immense edifice, supported on lofty columns, like a temple."

6- Covering

Its covering is no less than a clouded canopy or starry decked heaven, where all good Masons hope at last to arrive, by the aid of that theological ladder which Jacob, in his vision, saw ascending from earth to heaven, the three principal rounds of which are denominated *Faith*, *Hope*, and *Charity*, and which admonish us to have faith in God, hope of immortality, and charity to all humankind.

The greatest of these is Charity; for our Faith may be lost in sight; Hope ends in fruition, but Charity extends beyond the grave through the boundless realms of eternity.

The Lodge continues throughout this degree to be presented to the initiate as a symbol of the world. Hence, its covering is figuratively supposed to be the "clouded canopy" on which the host of stars is represented.

 If the Lodge represents the world, then its covering must be represented by the blue vault of heaven.

7- Furniture

The furniture of a Lodge consists of a Holy Bible, a Square, and Compasses. The Holy Bible is dedicated to God, the Square to the Master, and the Compasses to the Craft. The Bible is dedicated to God because it is the inestimable gift of God to man; * * * the Square to the Master because it is the proper Masonic emblem of his office; and the Compasses, to the craft, because, by due attention to their use, they are taught to circumscribe their desires, and keep their passions within due bounds.

8- Ornaments

The ornaments of a Lodge are the *Mosaic Pavement*, the *Indented Tessel*, and the *Blazing Star*. The Mosaic pavement represents the ground floor of King Solomon's Temple and the indented tessel, of that beautiful tesselated border or skirting surrounding it.

The Mosaic pavement is emblematical of human life, checkered with good and evil; the beautiful border which surrounds it is emblematical of those manifold blessings and comforts which surround us and which we hope to obtain by a faithful reliance on Divine Providence, which is hieroglyphically represented by the blazing star in the center.

Mosaic Pavements, consisting of stones of various colors, so disposed as to represent different shapes or forms, were common in the temples of the ancients.

Fellows said, *"that they represented the variegated face of the earth in the places where the ancients formerly held their religious assemblies."* The actual derivation of the word is unknown or at least unsettled.

The Indented Tessel is a border of stones of various colors placed around the pavement. *Tessel*, from the Latin *tessela*, means a little square stone, and to indent is to cut or notch a margin into inequalities resembling teeth. A *tesselated border* is, therefore, a notched border of variegated colors.

The Blazing Star is said by Webb to be "commemorative of the star which appeared to guide the wise men of the East to the place of our Savior's nativity."

This, one of the ancient interpretations of the symbol, being considered too sectarian in its character and unsuitable to the universal religion of Masonry, has been omitted since the meeting of Grand Lecturers at Baltimore in 1842.

9- Lights

A Lodge has three symbolic lights; one in the East, one in the West, and one in the South. There is no light in the north because King Solomon's Temple, of which every Lodge is a representation, was placed so far north of the ecliptic that the sun and moon, at their meridian height, could dart no rays into the northern part thereof.

The north we, therefore, masonically call a place of darkness. The three lights, like the three principal officers and the three principal supports, refer undoubtedly to the three stations of the sun—its rising in the east, its meridian in the south, and its setting in the west—and thus the symbolism of the Lodge, as typical of the world, continues to be preserved.

The use of lights in all religious ceremonies is an ancient custom. A seven-branched candlestick was in the tabernacle, and in the Temple "were the golden candlesticks, five on the right and five on the left." They were always typical of moral, spiritual, or intellectual light.

10- Jewels

A Lodge has six jewels; three are immovable, and three are movable. The immovable jewels are the *Square*, *Level*, and *Plumb*. The square inculcates morality; the level, equality; and the plumb, rectitude of conduct.

They are called immovable jewels because they are always to be found in the East, West, and South parts of the Lodge, being worn by the officers in those respective stations.

The movable jewels are the *Rough Ashlar*, the *Perfect Ashlar*, and the *Trestle-Board*.[9]The rough ashlar is a stone taken from the quarry in its rude and natural state.

The perfect ashlar is a stone made ready by the hands of the workmen to be adjusted by the working tools of the fellow craft.

The trestle board is for the master workman to draw his designs upon. By the rough ashlar, we are reminded of our rude and imperfect state by nature; by the perfect ashlar, that state of perfection at which we hope to arrive by a virtuous education, our endeavors, and the blessing of God.

By the trestle-board, we are also reminded that, as the operative workman erects his temporal building agreeably to the rules and designs laid down by the master on his trestle-board, so should we, both operative and speculative, endeavor to erect our spiritual building.

Agreeably to the rules and designs laid down by the Supreme Architect of the Universe, the great books of nature and revelation are our spiritual, moral, and masonic trestle-board.

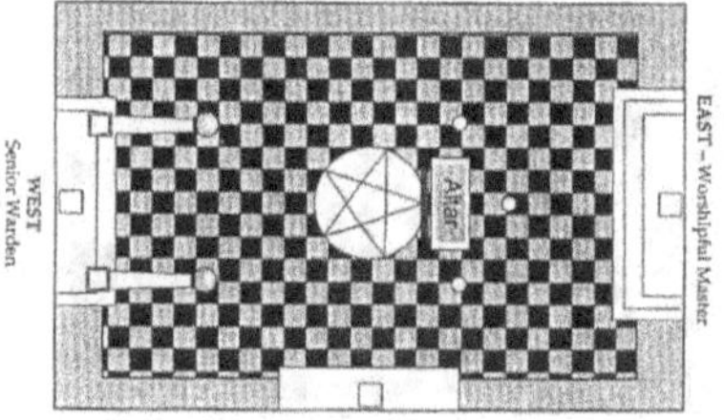

11- Situated

A Lodge is situated due east and west because when Moses crossed the Red Sea, being pursued by Pharaoh and his host, he erected on the other side, by divine command, a tabernacle, which he placed due east and west to receive the first rays of the rising sun and to commemorate that mighty east wind by which their miraculous deliverance was affected.

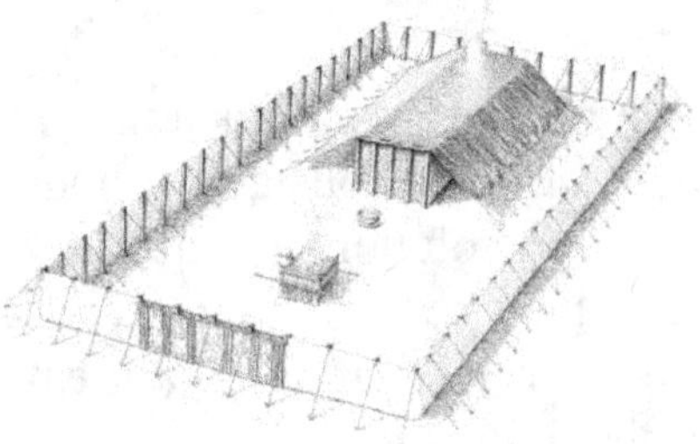

This tabernacle was an exact pattern of King Solomon's Temple, of which every Lodge is a representation, and it is, or ought, therefore, to be placed due east and west. The *orientation* of Lodges, or their position due east and west, is derived from the universal custom of antiquity.

"The heathen temples," says Dudley, "*were so constructed that their length was directed toward the east, and the entrance was by a portico at the western front, where the altar stood, so that the votaries approaching for the performance of religious rites, directed their faces toward the east, the quarter of sunrise.*"

The primitive reason for this custom undoubtedly is to be found in the early prevalence of sun worship, and hence the spot where that luminary first made his appearance in the heavens was consecrated, in the minds of his worshipers, as a place entitled to peculiar reverence.

Long after the reason had ceased, the custom continued to be observed. Christian churches still are built when circumstances permit, with particular reference to an east-and-west position.

Freemasonry, retaining in its symbolism the typical reference
of the Lodge to the world and constantly alluding to the sun
in his apparent diurnal revolution, imperatively required
when it can be done, that the Lodge should be situated due
east and west so that every ceremony shall remind the Mason
of the progress of that luminary.

12- Dedicated

Our ancient brethren dedicated their Lodges to King Solomon
because he was our first Most Excellent Grand Master, but
modern Masons dedicate theirs to St. John the Baptist and St.
John the Evangelist, who were two eminent patrons of
Masonry; and since their time, there is represented,
in every regular and well-covered Lodge, a specific point
within a circle, embordered by two perpendicular parallel lines,
representing St. John the Baptist and St. John the Evangelist, and
upon the top rests the Holy Scriptures.

The point represents an individual brother; the circle is the boundary line beyond which he will never suffer his prejudices or passions to betray him.

In going around this circle, we necessarily touch upon these two lines and the Holy Scriptures. While a Mason keeps himself circumscribed within these due bounds, it is impossible that he should materially err.

The point within a circle is an interesting and important symbol in Freemasonry. Still, it has been so based on the interpretation given in the modern lectures that the sooner the Masonic student forgets that interpretation, the better it will be.

The symbol is a beautiful but mysterious allusion to the old sun worship. It introduces us to that modification known among the ancients as the worship of the Phallus. The Phallus was an imitation of the male generative organ.

It was usually represented by a column, surrounded by a circle at its base, intended for the *cteis*, or female generative organ.

This union of the ***phallus*** *(male organ)* and the ***cteis*** *(female organ),* which is well represented by the *point within the circle*, was intended by the ancients as a type of the prolific powers of nature, which they worshiped under the united form of the active or male principle, and the passive or female principle.

Impressed with this idea of the union of these two principles, they made the older of their deities hermaphrodite and supposed Jupiter or the Supreme God, to have within himself both sexes or, as one of their Poets expresses it, "to have been created a male and an unpolluted virgin.

"Now, this hermaphrodism of the Supreme Divinity was again supposed to be represented by the sun, the male generative energy, and by nature or the universe, which was the female prolific principle.

And this union was symbolized in different ways, but principally by the point within the circle, the point indicating the sun, and the circle the universe of nature, warmed into life by his prolific rays.

The two parallel lines, which in the modern lectures are said to represent St. John the Baptist and St. John the Evangelist, really allude to particular periods in the sun's annual course.

At two particular points in this course, the sun is found on the zodiacal signs Cancer and Capricorn, which are distinguished as the summer and winter solstice.

He has reached his greatest northern and southern limit when the sun is in these points. If the circle represents the sun's annual course, these points will be indicated by the points where the parallel lines touch the circle.

But the days when the sun reaches these points are the 21st of June and the 22nd of December, and this will account for their subsequent application to the two Saints, John, whose anniversaries the Church has placed near those days.

So, the true interpretation of the point within the circle is the same as that of the Master and Wardens of a Lodge. The reference to the symbolism of the world and the Lodge is preserved in both.

The Master and Wardens are symbols of the sun—the Lodge, of the universe or the world; the point also is the symbol of the same sun, and the surrounding circle of the universe, while the two parallel lines point, not to two saints, but to the two northern and southern limits of the sun's course.

Brotherly Love, Relief and Truth

13- Principal Tenents

The three great tenets of Mason's profession are *Brotherly Love*, *Relief*, and *Truth*, which are thus described:

BROTHERLY LOVE. By the exercise of brotherly love, we are taught to regard the whole human species as one family; the high and low, the rich and poor; who, as created by one Almighty Parent and inhabitants of the same planet, are to aid, support, and protect each other.

On this principle, Masonry unites men of every country, sect, and opinion and conciliates true friendship among those who might otherwise have remained at a perpetual distance.

RELIEF. To relieve the distressed is a duty incumbent on all men, particularly on Masons, who are linked together by an indissoluble chain of sincere affection.

To soothe the unhappy, to sympathize with their misfortunes, to compassionate their miseries, and to restore peace to their troubled minds, is the great aim we have in view. On this basis, we form our friendships and establish our connections.

TRUTH. Truth is a divine attribute and the foundation of every virtue. To be good and true is the first lesson in Masonry. On this theme, we contemplate and endeavor to regulate our conduct by its dictates.

Hence, while influenced by this principle, hypocrisy and deceit are unknown among us, sincerity and plain dealing distinguish us, and the heart and tongue join in promoting each other's welfare and rejoicing in each other's prosperity.

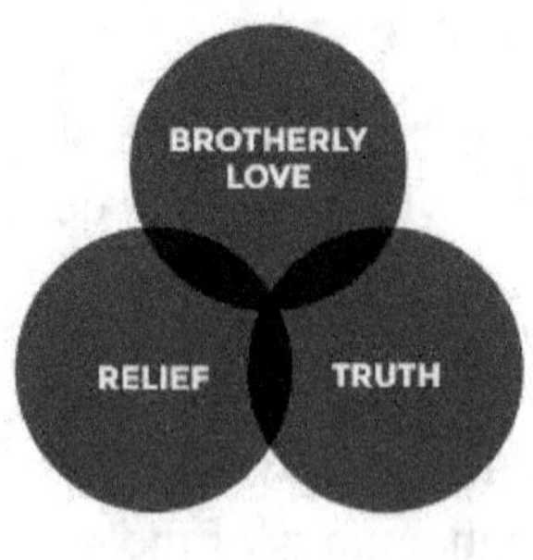

14- Cardinal Virtues

Every Mason has four perfect points, which are illustrated by the four cardinal virtues, T*emperance*, *Fortitude*, *Prudence*, and *Justice*, and are thus explained:

TEMPERANCE.

Temperance is that due restraint upon our affections and passions, which renders the body tame and governable and frees the mind from the allurements of vice.

This virtue should be the constant practice of every Man, as he is thereby taught to avoid excess, or contracting any immoral or malicious habit, the indulgence of which might lead him to disclose some of those valuable secrets which he has promised to conceal and never reveal, and which would consequently subject him to the contempt and detestation of all good Masons.

FORTITUDE.

Fortitude is that noble and steady purpose of the mind whereby we are unable to undergo any pain, peril, or danger when prudentially deemed expedient.

This virtue is equally distant from rashness and cowardice; and, like the former, should be deeply impressed upon the mind of every Mason as a safeguard or security against any illegal attack. That may be done, by force or otherwise, to extort from him any of those valuable secrets with which he has been so solemnly entrusted and which were emblematically represented upon his first admission into the Lodge.

PRUDENCE.

Prudence teaches us to regulate our lives and actions agreeably to the dictates of reason and is that habit by which we wisely judge and prudentially determine all things relative to our present and future happiness.

This virtue should be the peculiar characteristic of every Mason, not only for the government of his conduct while in the Lodge but also abroad. It should be mainly attended to in all strange and mixed companies, never to let fall the least sign, token, or word whereby the secrets of Masonry might be unlawfully obtained.

JUSTICE.

Justice is that standard, or boundary of right, which enables us to render to every man his just due, without distinction. This virtue is not only consistent with Divine and human laws but is the very cement and support of civil society, and as justice in a great measure constitutes the real good man, so should it be the invariable practice of every Mason never to deviate from the tiniest principles thereof.

15- Chalk (*freedom*), Charcoal (*fervency*) and Clay (*zeal*)

Entered Apprentices should serve their Masters with freedom, fervency, and zeal, emblematically represented by chalk, charcoal, and clay.

Nothing is freer than ___chalk,___ the slightest touch of which leaves a trace. Nothing is more fervent than charcoal, for the most obdurate metals will yield when properly ignited. There is nothing more zealous than ___clay,___ our mother earth, for it, alone of all the elements, has never proved unfriendly to man.

Through constantly harassed, more to furnish the luxuries than the necessaries of life, she never refuses her yield, strewing our pathway with flowers and spreading our table with plenty. Though she produces poison, she still furnishes the antidote and returns every good committed to her care with interest.

And when we are finally called upon to pass through the Valley of the Shadow of Death, she once more receives us and tenderly enfolds our remains within her bosom, thus admonishing us that, as from earth we came, so to earth, we must surely return.

"In participating in the ceremony of the First Degree, the Candidate receives, symbolically, a look into the nature of his own psyche. Suppose he gives serious attention to the work of his Lodge and tries to understand it in the way we have outlined. In that case, there will come (sooner or later) a moment when 'it all comes together," and he sees his interior being as the symbolism represents it.

When he has had such a look, in fact, when he has had a natural (not symbolic) experience which indicates that he is an individual, which proves to him that the thoughts he thinks and the decisions he takes have a real, tangible, usually immediate, effect on his life and the lives of others; when he has once had even a glimpse into the workings of his psyche, he can never forget it.

He cannot 'unsee' what he has seen; he can never put aside what that glimpse of his interior has taught him. A person with this sort of insight can, and should, remain committed to the well-being of others and the advancement of his society. But, just as the Rough Ashlar which has been cut from the quarry will then be an individual stone, such a person will be an individual, with personal responsibility for his actions and the situations in which he finds himself for as long as he lives". **(Carl H. Claudy)**

<u>Quiz</u>

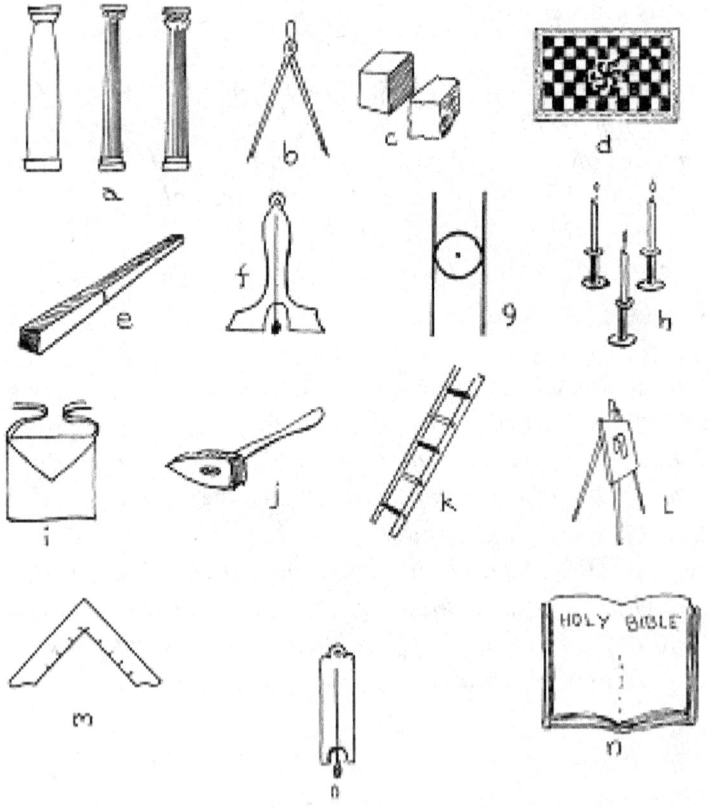

Reflecting on the Hidden Mysteries of Ancient Freemasonry (Psalms 133)

Behold, how good and how pleasant it is for brethren to dwell together in unity!

It is like the precious ointment upon the head that ran down upon the beard, even Aaron's beard, that went down to the skirts of his garments;

as the dew of Hermon, and as the dew that descended upon the mountains of Zion: for there the Lord commanded the blessing, even life forevermore.

Psalms 133

As an Entered Apprentice, I recall the first time I heard Psalms 133 as a mason—my impression of the first verse needed to be more precise and less confusing. On the one hand, there was a sense of calmness and unity among the men I met for the first time, and I did not know anything about them.

On the other hand, I had a sense of concern and doubts about my upcoming experience with men I did not know. To "dwell together in unity" or to be in the company of a group of men united in mind and spirit? This can either be a really good thing or a really bad thing.

The second verse I found more confusing than the first. It sounds like someone being consecrated or exalted to a priest or a religious position.

The third verse I found very interesting because it gave me an impression of a geographical location. I asked one of the brothers what was the meaning of that biblical passage?

His response did not help; in a rude and brash tone, he said, *"You do not need to know what it means; you just need to regurgitate it and stop asking so many questions."* At that moment, we knew he did not understand what was happening as a man or mason. He was a complete contradiction to what we were being taught.

I felt sorry for him because he could not see what was clear to us, that he was trying to sound masonic and appear skilled by repeating and using words in the wrong context and not knowing what many of these words meant.

I remember hearing my classmate saying under his breath, "So much for "peace and unity." Our conductor saw what had happened and immediately corrected the nonsense that the brother was creating, and he also corrected my classmate.

It then dawned on me that we missed the lesson of Ps 133 as a class. It is about a peaceful unity, which should be of the utmost importance to all Masons. Our conductor explained that the brother's response was done incorrectly and that he could have shown more brotherly love. However, we were equally wrong for passing judgment on a brother we did not know.

Our conductor then said something that struck a chord with me, forcing me to take a good look at myself. He said, "How can you behold something that "is good and pleasant if you do not know what it is to be good and pleasant." I decided to investigate Ps. 133. So, once again, I went into detective mode, once again.

<u>Merriam-Webster Dictionary</u> defines *"Behold"*: *1: to perceive through sight or apprehension : 2: to gaze upon: OBSERVE. "Good": (1): of a favorable character or tendency. "Pleasant" 1: having qualities that tend to give pleasure: AGREEABLE a pleasant day 2: having or characterized by pleasing manners, behavior, or appearance. "Unity"2a: a condition of harmony: ACCORD. 2b: continuity without deviation or change (as in purpose or action) "Dwelling": a shelter (such as a house) in which people live or living among.*

*Behold, how good and how pleasant it is for brethren to
dwell together in unity!*

This first sentence in Ps. 133 for the confraternization
(*con·fraternization: fraternization together: recognition as a
brother, Merriam-Webster Dictionary)* of the travelers that
spend the day gathered in the great path of the Temple.

People from all of Israel, who barely knew each other, from
all areas, congregated there as brothers and sisters, as
members of a great family of the same nation that lives under
the deep happiness of adoring only one God.

*"It is like the precious ointment upon the head, that ran down
upon the beard, even Aaron's beard, that went down to the
skirts of his garments...."*

God appointed Aaron, the older brother of Moses, and his
sons to be the High Priest and ministers of God for the
children of Israel (Exodus 28:1). God directed that an "oil of
holy ointment" (Exodus 30:23-25) be made consisting of
measured amounts of myrrh, sweet cinnamon, sweet calamus,
cassia, and olive oil.

This "holy anointing oil" was to be poured upon Aaron and
his sons as a blessing or consecration before their entry as
priests into the Tabernacle, containing all the holy vessels
and the Ark of the Covenant, to minister and pray unto the
Lord (Exodus 30:30). This reference, therefore, alludes to the
sacredness of such unity.

"As the dew of Hermon, and as the dew that descended upon the mountains of Zion: for there the Lord commanded the blessing, even life forevermore."

Mount Zion or Mount Hermon (Deuteronomy 4:48) was known to have abundant amounts of humidity, even in the driest weather, which formed on the tents so profusely that it appeared as though it had rained the whole night.

This precious dew or water provided continuous life-giving growth to the plants and animals of the otherwise waterless region, hence the allusion to life forevermore.

The Entered Apprentice Degree then, as explained to us by our conductor through this reference to this Scripture, is that we had entered a fraternal union with men of good character. This unity of good brethren is so precious that it is comparable to the holy anointing of the High Priest of the ancient Israelites.

His relationship with this fraternal unity promises to improve his future life just as the dew of Mount Hermon and the mountains of Zion.

Mount Hermon

Israel borders to the north with Lebanon and the west with Syria; Mount Hermon is the boundary among those countries. Because of its height, the mountain tops are permanently covered with snow in the desert regions; the evaporation of the humidity concentrates on the mountains and comes back during the night in the form of dew.

Because of the lack of rain, "the dew of Hermon" provides the environment for good crops. Additionally, the melting of Mount Hermon's snow is a source of nourishment for the Jordan River, which supplies the area with water for the soil.

Its benefit makes the crops a blessing for the people. So, in the vision of David, Mount Hermon, using its dew, is a sign of life.

Mount Zion

Mount Zion is a hill in Jerusalem, located just outside the walls of the Old City. The term Mount Zion has been used in the Hebrew Bible first for the City of David and later for the Temple Mount, but its meaning has shifted, and it is now used as the name of ancient Jerusalem's Western Hill.

It is approximately 2,510 feet in altitude, therefore the expression *"...to go down on Zion"* or *"on the hills of Zion"* because in Psalms 87:2 and 51:18, and more times in the Bible are found references where Jerusalem is called Zion.

In the psalm 125:1-2 there is a beautiful reference to this respect, as one can read:

*"The ones that trust the Lord are like Mount Zion that is not affected but remains forever. As the hills persist around Jerusalem, like this, the Lord stays around his people **from now, and forever**". (even life forevermore)*

When David conquered the fortress of Zion, he carried the
Ark of the Covenant to the fortress and built for it a
Tabernacle. Since then, Zion has become "the city of the
Lord," a place of His dwelling, a place for His rest.
"...this is my rest forever; here I will inhabit, for I wanted it
(Psalm 132:13-14).

With the presence of the Ark of the Covenant, Zion became
the religious capital of the Israelites, a holy place, sacred, as
inferred from the reading of Psalm 135:21, which tells us:
"...blessed be the Lord from Zion, that inhabits Jerusalem".

Final reflection on Ps. 133

David compares the oil descending on the head of Aaron with
the dew falling on Zion. Aaron is the supreme priest and the
religious chief of the Israeli nation; he is the spiritual "head"
of the Hebrew people, in the same way that Zion is the
spiritual capital of Israel.

When Aaron is purified and consecrated as the priest for the
service of the Lord, thus making Aaron the man pure, fair,
and perfect for the priestly functions, the dew on Zion is the
water that, besides purifying, makes possible the life around
Jerusalem.

It is like the oil (water) falling on Aaron (Jerusalem) because
there, in Zion, the Lord (represented by the Ark of the
Covenant) had ordered his blessing forever.

The fact of the pilgrims' being in that place, gathered, made it possible that the blessing, besides purifying, went down for all. It shows itself in nature, in the oil, in the dew, in the rains, in the Jordan River's waters, which irrigates the land and makes it fertile, making the Promised Land ownership possible.

David uses functional language to show that Zion is the religious center of Israel because that was the place the Lord had chosen for His home.

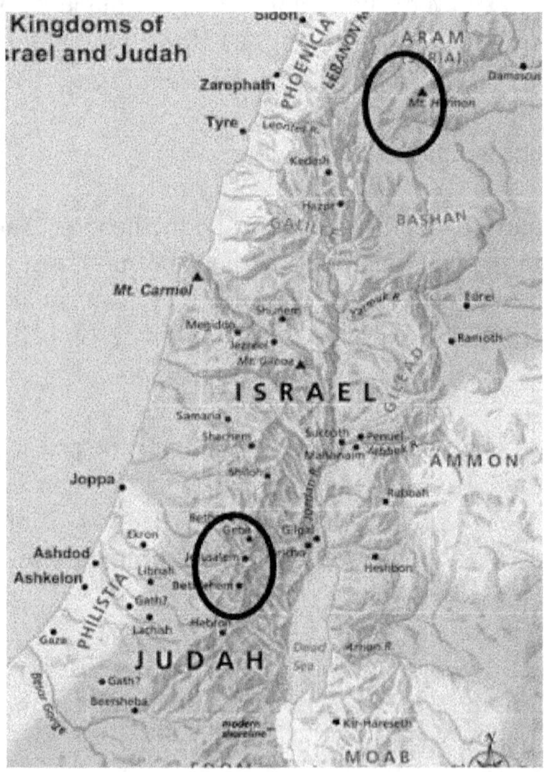

Reflecting on the Hidden Mysteries of Ancient Freemasonry (Boaz "Book of Ruth)

Boaz *(Book of Ruth)*

Reflecting on the Book of Ruth, I recall getting a phone call from my conductor, who congratulated me on being accepted into masonry. He informed me that before I got initiated, I needed to read the Book of Ruth, 1st and 2nd Kings, and 1st and 2nd Samuel. Become very familiar with the characters in these biblical stories.

As I started reading the book of Ruth, I must admit I was genuinely puzzled. I was under the impression that masonry was a male organization. I specifically remember thinking very naively, *"Was Ruth a Mason?"* "Why would he have me read a book about a woman?"

As I continued reading, it dawned on me that this story was about a woman and a man; now, I was really thrown for a loop! I read the book a second and third time.

So, once again, I went into detective mode.

<u>Merriam-Webster Dictionary</u> defines "Ruth" 1a: compassion for the misery of another, 1b: sorrow for one's own faults: Ruth 2a: a Moabite woman who accompanied Naomi to Bethlehem and became the ancestress of David, 2b: a short narrative book of canonical Jewish and Christian Scriptures.

*<u>Israelbiblecenter.com/ruth-Boaz-meaning-hebrew</u>- Although Ruth begins with emptiness, the story gradually begins to refill the lives of its protagonists. Tragically, Naomi is left without a husband or sons, but "Ruth" (רות) likely comes from the Hebrew word for **"companionship"** (רעות; re'ut), so that Naomi continues to have a loyal friend after the loss of her family.*

*More, one of the probable meanings of Boaz—the man who redeems Naomi and Ruth—is **"In Strength"** (בעז), which alludes to the strength of God to bring redemption out of tragedy. Therefore, while some of the names in Ruth serve to underscore initial emptiness, other names—like Ruth and Boaz—remind the reader of God's ongoing provision and the divine desire for the ultimate good.*

Amplified Bible Version *(biblehub.com) 1 Kings 7:21*
*"Hiram set up the pillars at the porch of the temple; he set up the left pillar and named it **Boaz** (in it is strength). By naming the pillar Boaz (1 Kings 7:21), the builders of the Temple indicated their view of Boaz as a symbol of strength.*

My reflections on the book of Ruth. Boaz, whose name means "Strength," was the son of Salmah or Salmon of the tribe of Judah and was a wealthy landowner near Bethlehem in the time of the Judges. During a famine around Bethlehem, a relative of Boaz, Elimelech, took his wife, Naomi, and his two sons, Mahlon and Chiilon, to the land of Moab.

There, Elimelech died, and his sons married Moabite women, contrary to Israelite custom. Both sons died, leaving the wives as widows and their mother-in-law, Naomi. Naomi decided to return to her people and told her daughters-in-law to remain with their fellow Moabites. However, Ruth, the widow of Mahlon, insisted upon accompanying Naomi, saying, *"Intreat me not to leave thee ... for whither thou goest, I will go ... thy people shall be my people, and thy God my God."*

Naomi took Ruth with her when she returned to Bethlehem. The death of her husband and sons had left Naomi bitter, but the devotion of Ruth eased her bitterness and renewed her interest in life.

Naomi's people also noticed Ruth's love and approved despite their bias against Moabites, stating that Ruth had become more to Naomi than seven sons. Still, they regarded Ruth as a Moabite rather than one of them, although she had adopted their religion.

Naomi sent Ruth to glean in the fields of Boaz, the wealthy kinsman of Naomi's late husband. Boaz saw her there and treated her kindly, commenting on her devotion to Naomi.

From this beginning, events develop until Ruth, at Naomi's urging, asks Boaz for his protection of her by marrying her. Israelite law placed the duty of right of protecting widows by marriage on the closest male relative of the deceased. As a Moabite, Ruth probably fell outside the duty of protection, although her late husband's nearest relative retained the right to assume that responsibility.

Boaz indicated his willingness to marry her but pointed out that a closer relative had a prior claim. Boaz went to that relative, whose name is not given, and asked whether or not he intended to assert his claim.

The relative relinquished his claim, leaving Ruth free to marry Boaz. One tradition state that Boaz was 80 years old and Ruth 40 when they married; he died the day after the wedding.

This may be a legend, but brief, their marriage produced a son, Obed, who became King David's grandfather.

The ancestry of David, and eventually of Joseph, the husband of Mary, the mother of Jesus, thus included Ruth, a Moabite woman, through her marriage to Boaz.

As I continue to reflect, the Story of Ruth and Boaz is speculative and operative, character and behavior, duty and responsibility, loyalty and humility, inspiring and examples, moral and virtuous. These traditions are in masonic goals and objectives that will eventually connect the body and soul.

Sources and References

Encyclopedia Britannica
The Holy Bible
Biblestudy.org
Bro. Antônio Guilherme de Paiva 33°
Pietre-Stone
Merriam- Webster's Dictionary
Mackey's Encyclopedia
Macoy's Cyclopedia
Albert Pikes Morals and Dogmas
Charles A. Claudy
Robert G. Davis
George H. Steinmetz
Robert V Lund

Special Thanks and Honorable Mention to

Honorable
Bro. Carlos Bazaldua

COMING SOON

The Masonic Reflection Series
Vol. 2 The Fellow Craft
Reflections of a Fellow Craft
CEDAR
STONE
METAL
Bro. Tony Pedroza 33°
"The Quarryman"